CONTENTS

KT-440-463

To the student   5
To the teacher   5
Thanks   5

EHWLC LEARNING CENTRE
EALING GREEN

WITHDRAWN

English Grammar in Use Supplementary Exercises

WITH ANSWERS

Louise Hashemi
with **Raymond Murphy**

EG31150

CAMBRIDGE
UNIVERSITY PRESS

PUBLISHED BY THE PRESS SYNDICATE OF THE UNIVERSITY OF CAMBRIDGE
The Pitt Building, Trumpington Street, Cambridge, United Kingdom

CAMBRIDGE UNIVERSITY PRESS
The Edinburgh Building, Cambridge CB2 2RU, UK   http://www.cup.cam.ac.uk
40 West 20th Street, New York, NY 10011–4211, USA   http://www.cup.org
10 Stamford Road, Oakleigh, Melbourne 3166, Australia
Ruiz de Alarcón 13, 28014 Madrid, Spain

© Cambridge University Press 1995

This book is in copyright. Subject to statutory exception
and to the provisions of relevant collective licensing agreements,
no reproduction of any part may take place without
the written permission of Cambridge University Press.

First published by Cambridge University Press 1995
Ninth printing 2000

Printed in the United Kingdom at the University Press, Cambridge

A catalogue record for this book is available from the British Library

ISBN 0 521 44954 5 English Grammar in Use Supplementary Exercises (with answers)
ISBN 0 521 44955 3 English Grammar in Use Supplementary Exercises (without answers)
ISBN 0 521 43680 X English Grammar in Use (with answers)
ISBN 0 521 43681 8 English Grammar in Use (without answers)

EHWLC LEARNING CENTRE
EALING GREEN

115829
425.

425.076 HAS

3 wk Main

TO THE STUDENT

This book is for intermediate and more advanced students who want extra practice in grammar. It covers most of the grammar areas in *English Grammar in Use*. You can use it without a teacher.

The book has 158 exercises. Each exercise relates to a particular part of *English Grammar in Use*. You can find the *English Grammar in Use* unit numbers in the top right-hand corner of each page. You can use this book if you don't have *English Grammar in Use* because all the answers, with lots of alternatives, are given in the Key (pages 113–126). But if you want an explanation of the grammar points, you'll need to check in *English Grammar in Use*.

The grammar points covered in the book are *not* in order of difficulty, so you can go straight to the parts where you need most practice. Where there are several exercises on one grammar point, however, you will find that the easier ones come first. It is a good idea to try one exercise, check your answers and then go on to the next one.

Many of the exercises are in the form of letters, conversations or short articles. You may like to use these as models for writing or speaking practice.

TO THE TEACHER

English Grammar in Use Supplementary Exercises offers extra practice of most of the grammar covered in *English Grammar in Use*. Much of the language is contextualised within dialogues, letters, articles etc., encouraging students to consider meaning as well as form. The book can be used as self-study material or as a basis for further practice in class or as homework.

It is designed for students who have already worked through the exercises in *English Grammar in Use* (or elsewhere) which are relevant to their needs, but who need more, or more challenging, practice. It is particularly useful for revision work.

The exercises are organised in the same order as the units of *English Grammar in Use*, and the numbers of the relevant *English Grammar in Use* units are shown in the top right-hand corner of each page. Although the grammar areas are not covered in order of difficulty in the book as a whole, there is a progression where several exercises are offered on one area. For example, exercise 8 requires the students to choose between given forms, exercise 9 requires them to put given verbs into the correct form, exercise 10 requires them to choose a verb and put it in the correct tense and exercise 11 requires them to supply a verb and put it in the correct tense. The contextualised practice in the book offers the opportunity for much further practice, using the exercises as models or springboards for speaking and writing practice of a freer nature.

THANKS

For trying out exercises, and offering valuable comments: students and staff at The British Council Young Learners' Centre, Barcelona, Spain; Anglo World, Cambridge; The Studio School, Cambridge; The International Language Academy, Cambridge; Lelio Pallini, Jon Butt, Cemille Iskenderoglu, Isidro Almendárez, Catherine Carpenter, Marco Palladino.

For both encouragement and practical support, at the Cambridge University Press: Jeanne McCarten, Geraldine Mark, Nóirín Burke, Nick Newton and Peter Ducker.

Present continuous and present simple
(*I am doing* and *I do*)

1   *Choose the correct form of the verbs.*

Dear Karen,

(1) <u>I'm having</u> / ~~I have~~ a great time here in England. My university term
(2) ~~isn't starting~~ / <u>doesn't start</u> until the autumn, so (3) <u>I'm taking</u> / I take the
opportunity to improve my English. (4) <u>I'm staying</u> / I stay with some English friends
who (5) ~~are owning~~ / <u>own</u> a farm. On weekdays (6) I'm catching / <u>I catch</u> a bus into
Torquay to go to language classes. (7) I'm making / <u>I make</u> good progress, I think. My
friends (8) <u>say</u> / are saying my pronunciation is much better than when I arrived, and
(9) I'm understanding / <u>I understand</u> almost everything now. At weekends
(10) <u>I'm helping</u> / I help on the farm. At the moment (11) <u>they're harvesting</u> / they
harvest the corn and (12) they're needing / <u>they need</u> all the help they can get. It's quite
hard work, but (13) I'm liking / <u>I like</u> it. And (14) <u>I'm developing</u> / I develop some strong
muscles!

(15) Do you come / <u>Are you coming</u> to visit me at Christmas? (16) <u>I'm spending</u> /
I spend the winter holiday here at the farm. My friends (17) are wanting / <u>want</u> to meet
you and there's plenty of space. But you must bring your warmest clothes. (18) <u>It's getting</u>
/ It gets very cold here in the winter.

Let me know as soon as (19) you're deciding / <u>you decide</u>. And tell me what
(20) <u>you're doing</u> / you do these days.

Do you miss me?

Love,

Paul

2   *Choose words from the box and make sentences as shown. Use a verb in the present continuous
and any other words you need.*

~~My boyfriend~~   I   My father   ~~My sister~~   ~~My classmates~~   My family   Our teacher   My boss   None of my friends   Several of my colleagues   Our next door neighbour   My best friend   My wife   Our children

1   My boyfriend <u>'s studying for his final exams</u> this term.
2   My sister <u>is working at home</u> this week.
3   My classmates <u>aren't talking much</u> right now.
4   .... this year.
5   .... at the moment.
6   .... this year.
7   .... this week.
8   .... this term.
9   .... right now.

3   *Put the verbs in the correct tense, present simple or present continuous.*

Leila Markham is an environmentalist. She is being interviewed on the radio by Tony Hunt, a journalist.

TONY: So tell me, Leila, why is it important to save the rainforests?

LEILA: There are a number of reasons. One is that many plants which could be useful in medicine (1) ..grow.. (grow) in the rainforest. We (2) ..don't know.. (not / know) all the plants yet – there are thousands and thousands of them. Researchers (3) .are trying. (try) to discover their secrets before they are destroyed.

TONY: I see. What other reasons are there?

LEILA: Well, I'm sure you've heard of global warming?

TONY: You mean, the idea that the world (4) .... (get) warmer?

LEILA: That's right. The rainforests (5) .... (have) an important effect on the earth's climate. They (6) .... (disappear) at a terrifying rate and soon they will be gone. People (7) .... (not / do) enough to save them.

TONY: But is global warming really such a problem? I (8) .... (enjoy) warm sunshine.

LEILA: Well, what (9) .... (happen) when you (10) .... (heat) ice?

TONY: It (11) .... (melt) of course.

LEILA: OK. The polar ice caps (12) .... (consist) of millions of tons of ice. If they (13) .... (melt), the level of the sea will rise and cause terrible floods. Many scientists (14) .... (believe) that temperatures (15) .... (already rise). We must do everything we can to prevent global warming, and that (16) .... (include) preserving the rainforests!

TONY: Thank you, Leila, and good luck in your campaign.

LEILA: Thank you.

Past simple and past continuous (*I did* and *I was doing*)   **Units 5 and 6**

4   *Use the words given to make sentences to match the pictures. Do not change the order of the words. Use only the past simple or past continuous.*

1

Cathy / phone / the post office / when the parcel / arrive
Cathy phoned the post office when the parcel arrived.

2

when Don / arrive / we / have / coffee
When Don arrived we were having coffee.

3

Henry

while he / walk / in the mountains /
Henry / see / a bear

Henry see Bear while
he walk in the
mountains.

4

the students / play / a game / when
the professor / arrive

the professor arrive
when the students
play a game

5

Felix

*Is that the Fire
Brigade?*

Felix / phone / the fire brigade /
when the cooker / catch / fire

Felix phone fought to fire
brigade when the cooker
catched

6

when the starter / fire / his pistol /
the race / begin — began.

7

I / walk / home / when it / start / to
rain

I was walking home when it
start to

8

Margaret

when Margaret / open / the door /
the phone / ring

9

Cora / read / a letter / when Jimmy /
phone / her

....
....
....

10

Andy / come / out of the restaurant /
when he / see / Jenny

....
....
....

5   *Choose the correct form of the verbs.*

THOMAS EDISON (1) <u>started</u>/~~was starting~~ work
on the railway when he was twelve, selling
newspapers and snacks. There were long periods
with nothing for him to do so he
(2) <u>built/was building</u> himself a little laboratory
in the luggage van where he could carry out
experiments when he (3) <u>didn't sell/wasn't
selling</u> things to passengers. Another way that he (4) <u>occupied/was occupying</u> himself
was by reading. He joined a library and (5) <u>read/was reading</u> every single book in it.
One day, when he (6) <u>waited/was waiting</u> at a station he (7) <u>noticed/was noticing</u> a small
boy who (8) <u>played/was playing</u> by the track, unaware that a train (9) <u>approached/was
approaching</u>. Edison (10) <u>ran/was running</u> out and (11) <u>grabbed/was grabbing</u> the child
just in time. The child's father was so grateful that he (12) <u>offered/was offering</u> to teach
Edison to be a telegraph operator. Edison accepted the offer and soon he (13) <u>had/was
having</u> regular lessons. After a year, he was good enough to get a job in the telegraph
office. He continued to read and experiment, whenever he (14) <u>had/was having</u> time. At
twenty-one he (15) <u>left/was leaving</u> the telegraph office to devote all his time to being an
inventor. He (16) <u>went/was going</u> on to invent the electric light bulb, the phonograph and
the movie camera.

6 *Complete this description of the life of a musician, using the verbs given. Use either the past simple or the past continuous.*

Colin Boyle was born in 1973 near Dublin, Ireland. In 1983 he became seriously ill. While he
(1) **was recovering** (recover) his uncle (2) **gave** (give) him an old violin. He enjoyed playing and
practised at his school every day after lessons. One day in 1987, John Leaf, the manager of
several successful musicians, (3) .... (have) a meeting with the
headmaster when he (4) .... (hear) Colin practising. He immediately
(5) .... (contact) Colin's teacher and (6) .... (invite)
Colin to appear in one of the concerts he (7) .... (organise) that year.
Colin, however, (8) .... (refuse) Leaf's invitation, because just then he
(9) .... (prepare) for some important school exams. Colin
(10) .... (pass) his exams and (11) .... (go) to
college to study engineering. At college he (12) .... (meet) Kim O'Malley,
who (13) .... (study) chemistry. Kim was also a keen amateur musician.
Being students, they rarely (14) .... (have) much money and they usually
(15) .... (work) as waiters at weekends. One evening in April 1992, while
Colin and Kim (16) .... (serve) customers, the manager
(17) .... (announce) that there would be no live music in the restaurant
that night as the regular band could not come. Colin and Kim (18) ....
(persuade) him to let them play to the customers. Everyone (19) .... (be)
amazed to hear how good they (20) .... (be). Six months later they
(21) .... (decide) to leave college because they (22) ....
(earn) so much money as musicians. Their success has continued ever since.

7 *Complete the following paragraphs with suitable verbs. Use either the past simple or past continuous tense.*

A John Blake was born in London in 1969. He (1) **went** to work in France when he was nineteen.
While he (2) .... in a restaurant in Paris, he (3) ....
Luisa, an Italian student. He (4) .... her to marry him, but she
wouldn't. Heartbroken, he (5) .... to England. Three years later, John
(6) .... along a street in London when he (7) ....
Luisa. She (8) .... London with a friend called Maria. When John and
Maria (9) ...., they fell in love at first sight, and got married the
following year.

B I had a terrible time last Saturday. It was rather cold, but quite sunny, so after lunch I
(10) **walked** into town. I (11) .... to buy a pullover. I
(12) .... in the window of a clothes shop when someone
(13) .... my wallet. While I (14) .... home, it
(15) .... to rain and I arrived home cold and miserable. I
(16) .... to have a hot bath. I (17) .... ready to
have my bath when the doorbell (18) .... It was a salesman and it took
me several minutes to get rid of him. Unfortunately, all the time he (19) ....
to me the water (20) .... You can imagine the state of the bathroom!

Now complete this paragraph, using the pictures to help you.

C We had a great time last weekend. It (21) ..was a lovely day.., so in the evening we
(22) ..cycled into town... We (23) .... a pizza.
We (24) .... the menu when a waiter (25) ....
me. While the manager (26) ...., another waiter (27) ....
.... my friend. Of course, we (28) ....
the meal.

Present continuous and present simple; past continuous and past simple (*I am doing* and *I do*; *I was doing* and *I did*)

8 *Choose the correct form of the verbs.*

ADAM: Hello, Mike. What (1) <u>are you doing</u> / <s>do you do</s> in this part of London?

MIKE: Well, actually, (2) <u>I'm looking</u> / <s>I look</s> at flats round here.

ADAM: Flats? (3) <u>Are you wanting</u> / <u>Do you want</u> to move?

MIKE: Yes, in fact, believe it or not, Mandy and I (4) <u>are getting</u> / <u>get</u> married.

ADAM: That's great! Congratulations. When (5) <u>were you deciding</u> / <u>did you decide</u>?

MIKE: Only last week. It was while we (6) <u>were staying</u> / <u>stayed</u> with her family in Scotland.
Now (7) <u>we try</u> / <u>we're trying</u> to find a suitable flat.

ADAM: It'll be great to have you as neighbours. I hope you manage to buy one soon.

MIKE: Oh we (8) <u>aren't looking</u> / <u>don't look</u> for one to buy. We (9) <u>aren't having</u> / <u>don't have</u>
enough money yet. (10) <u>We're wanting</u> / <u>We want</u> to find somewhere to rent.

ADAM: Yes, of course. That's what we (11) <u>did</u> / <u>were doing</u> at first. Actually, in the end, my
brother (12) <u>was lending</u> / <u>lent</u> us some money. That's how we (13) <u>were managing</u> /
<u>managed</u> to buy ours.

MIKE: Really? Perhaps I'll talk to my family before (14) <u>we choose</u> / <u>we're choosing</u> a flat.

ADAM: That's not a bad idea. My family (15) <u>gave</u> / <u>were giving</u> us quite a lot of helpful advice.
Now, what about a coffee? There's a good place just round the corner.

MIKE: Oh, yes, I (16) <u>looked</u> / <u>was looking</u> for somewhere to sit down when I bumped into you.
Let's go.

9   *Complete each sentence with a suitable form of the verb given. Use the present simple or continuous, or the past simple or continuous.*

1   I remember the day you got engaged. We ..*were having*.. tea in the garden when you came out of the house and told us. (have)
2   I tried to explain the situation to my parents, but they just .... what I was talking about. (not / understand)
3   What have you put in this sauce? It .... absolutely disgusting. (taste)
4   Peter always claimed that he was innocent, but for many years no one .... him. (believe)
5   It's a lovely shawl, I know, but unfortunately it .... to me. I'm just borrowing it for the party this evening. (not / belong)
6   Why .... that thin dress? You'll freeze to death in this cold wind! (you / wear)
7   Molly's fed up because she injured her ankle when she .... this morning, so she can't dance. (jog)
8   While I was admiring the view, someone stole the bag which .... all my traveller's cheques. (contain)
9   Look! .... that man standing beside the cash desk? I'm sure he's planning to steal something. (you / see)
10 Tea or coffee? I'm making both, so just say which you .... (prefer)
11 The boys didn't want to come shopping with us because they .... the football on television. (watch)

10   *Use the verbs in the box to complete the following dialogue. Use the present simple or continuous, or the past simple or continuous. Read the whole conversation before you start.*

> ~~do~~   give   go   have   ~~revise~~   see   shake   try   not / go   not / use   ~~not / work~~

Fred is phoning his friend Jane.

FRED: Hello, Jane, it's Fred here.
JANE: Oh, hello Fred. What (1) ..*are you doing*..?
FRED: Nothing much. I (2) ..*was revising*.. but I had to stop because my computer (3) ..*isn't working*...
JANE: Oh dear. Well, I (4) .... mine. Would you like to come and borrow it?
FRED: Thanks, but I'd rather go out. Would you like to come to the cinema? They (5) .... two tickets for the price of one this afternoon.
JANE: What's on?
FRED: I'm not sure.
JANE: Well, I (6) .... if I don't know what film we'll see.
FRED: Wait a minute. I (7) .... to find the right page in the newspaper. Oh, it's a horror film. How about it?
JANE: Definitely not. You know I (8) .... nightmares when I (9) .... horror films. We (10) .... to see one last year and by the end I (11) .... with terror.
FRED: Oh, all right. Well, see you on Monday I suppose.
JANE: Yes, OK. Bye.
FRED: Bye.

11   *Fill the gaps in this letter with suitable verbs. Use the present simple or continuous, or the past simple or continuous.*

Dear Anita,
    Thank you for your entertaining letter, which (1) ...**arrived**.. *yesterday. I* (2) ..**am beginning**.. *to feel much better now although my leg still* (3) .... *if I* (4) ....
too far. Last weekend I (5) .... *some friends who* (6) ....
their summer holidays just up the road from here. They're very nice – I hope you'll meet them if you come here next month. I (7) .... *to their house quite easily, but while I*
(8) .... *home, my leg* (9) .... *to ache really badly.*
So this week I (10) .... *more careful.*
    I'm very pleased you (11) .... *to find that book about Indian music that you* (12) .... *for. I have some cassettes you can borrow if you* (13) ....
I must stop now, because I (14) .... *rather tired.*
    Please write again and send me some books. This is a lovely place, but you know me, I
(15) .... *bored very quickly!*
    With much love,
    Alice

12   *Most of these sentences contain one mistake. Correct each one or, if there is no mistake, write* **right**.

1   The coffee is smelling wonderful. ...**smells wonderful.**...
2   Last year we visited the States. ...**RIGHT**.......
3   The ship sank because the engineer wasn't calling for help until it was already sinking.
    ....
4   The reason I get fat is that I'm always tasting things while I'm cooking. ....
5   How is Jennifer? Does her health improve? ....
6   You're quite right, I'm completely agreeing with you. ....
7   What did you after you left school? ....
8   Now I understand what you're trying to say! ....
9   I can't imagine why you were believing all those rumours. ....
10   Martin looked forward to a peaceful weekend, when his brother arrived with all his friends from the football club. ....
11   Philippa heard the result of the election as she was driving to work, so she phoned me when she got there. ....
12   Oh, I'm so sorry, I've spilt some tea. Where are you keeping the paper towels? ....
    ....

Present perfect simple and continuous
(*I have done* and *I have been doing*)

13 *Complete the following conversation with verbs from the box. Use the present perfect simple or continuous. You will need to use some of the verbs more than once. Read the whole conversation before you start.*

> be   come   do   drive   find   have   look   manage

Jane is being interviewed by Mrs Carr for a job working with young children.

MRS CARR: Come in Jane, do take a seat. Would you like a coffee?

JANE: Thank you, actually I (1) ...'ve just had... (just) one.

MRS CARR: Oh good. Now, do you know this area at all?

JANE: Quite well. My grandparents live just on the outskirts of town so I (2) .... here for holidays since I was little. I'm staying with them at the moment, actually.

MRS CARR: Oh, that's nice. And do you have a driving licence?

JANE: Yes. I (3) .... for four years now.

MRS CARR: And would you say you're a careful driver?

JANE: Yes, I think so. At least I (4) .... (never) an accident.

MRS CARR: Good. Now, could you tell me why you think you would be right for this job?

JANE: Well, I (5) .... (always) interested in working with small children. And I (6) .... to get quite a bit of practical experience by taking holiday jobs and so on.

MRS CARR: How do you think you would cope in an emergency?

JANE: I'm quite a calm person, I think. I (7) .... a first aid course, too. I got this badge.

MRS CARR: Oh, yes. That's good. Now, this job isn't permanent, as you know. We need someone for about a year. How would that fit with your long-term plans?

JANE: I'd like to work abroad eventually. But I want some full-time experience first. I (8) .... a Nursery Teacher's course this year. We finish next week, in fact, and I've already got a Child Care certificate.

MRS CARR: Well, I can't make any promises, but you do sound just the sort of person we're looking for. When would you be able to start?

JANE: As soon as I finish my Nursery Teacher's course.

MRS CARR: Excellent. And would you live with your grandparents?

JANE: Well, they live a bit far away. I'd probably try to get a small flat. I (9) .... in the paper every day, but I (10) .... (not) anything yet.

MRS CARR: Well, if you get the job, we'll try to help you. Now, would you like to come and meet some of the children?

JANE: Oh, yes.

MRS CARR: Right, if you'll just follow me then ...

14 Complete the responses to the following remarks and questions according to the information in the pictures. Use the present perfect simple or continuous.

1

EARLIER THIS MORNING

EXAM IN PROGRESS

NOW

You look dreadfully tired.

Yes, I am. I've been doing an exam all morning.

2

ABOUT NOW

WELCOME to NEW YORK

ARRIVALS

now

Isn't your brother here?

Sorry, no. He's gone to New York.

3

EARLIER TODAY

NOW

You're looking very smart!

*Thanks, I ....
......................*

4

A FEW MINUTES AGO

NOW

Why are you crying?

*Don't worry. It's only because I ....
......................*

5

EARLIER THIS WEEK

FOR SALE

NOW

Can you give me a lift to work?

*I'm afraid I can't. You see, I ....
......................*

6

A MOMENT AGO

NOW

Why do you want the antiseptic?

*Because I ....
....
......................*

→

15

15   *Use the words given to complete the sentences. Put the verbs in the present perfect simple or continuous.*

1   John's terribly upset. **He's broken**... (he / break) off his engagement to Megan. Apparently
    she's been seeing.. (she / see) someone else while **he's been**. (he / be) in Africa.

2   Can you translate this note from Stockholm? I understood Swedish when I was a child, but
    .... (I / forget) it all.

3   What's that dent in the side of the car? .... (you / have)
    an accident?

4   I'm sorry, John's not here; .... (he / go) the dentist.
    .... (he / have) trouble with a tooth.

5   This cassette recorder is broken. .... (you / play about) with it?

6   Your Italian is very good. .... (you / study) it long?

7   Do you mind if I clear the table? .... (you / have)
    enough to eat?

8   I'm not surprised .... (he / fail) that exam.
    .... (he / not / work) hard recently.

9   Oh no! .... (the children / cook). Look at the state of
    this kitchen!

10   How many times .... (Wendy / be) late for work this week?

11   I'm going to give that cat some food. .... (it / sit) on
    the doorstep for hours. I'm sure it's starving.

12   .... (I / do) grammar exercises all morning. I deserve a
    treat for lunch.

13   .... (you / not / buy) your mother a present? That's
    really mean of you!

14   I saw Katie yesterday. .... (she / work) in Australia
    for the past year. Did you know?

15   Now where are my keys? This is the third time .... (I / lose)
    them today!

16   .... (you / ever / play) chess? You should try it. I'm
    sure it's the sort of game you'd like.

17   Oh do be quiet. .... (you / grumble) all day!

18   .... (your tennis / really / improve)!
    .... (you / practise) in secret?

Present perfect simple and continuous, and simple past

(*I have done, I have been doing* and *I did*)

Units 7–10

16   *Rewrite each of the following sentences without changing the meaning, beginning in the way shown. You may need to use the present perfect or the simple past.*

1   We haven't been to a concert for over a year.
    The last time ..we went to a concert was over a year ago...
2   Your birthday party was the last time I really enjoyed myself.
    I ....
3   It's nearly twenty years since my father saw his brother.
    My father ....
4   James went to Scotland last Friday and is still there.
    James has ....
5   When did you last ride a bike?
    How long is it .... ?
6   The last time I went swimming was when we were in Spain.
    I haven't ....
7   You haven't tidied this room for weeks.
    It's ....

Present perfect and present

(*I have done / I have been doing* and *I do / I am doing*)

Units 7–12

17   *Complete the sentences with one of the verbs in the box in a suitable form. Be careful – some of them are negative.*

be	~~deal~~	~~finish~~	know	have
make	see	speak	stare	suffer
suit	want	seem		

1   I'm afraid I ..haven't finished.. typing those letters. I ..'ve been dealing... with customers all morning.
2   That jacket really .... you. How long .... you
    .... your own clothes?
3   Thank you, but I really .... any more juice.
    I .... two large glasses already.
4   I can't find my watch. .... you .... it recently?
5   Paul .... from earache since the weekend.
    He .... to the doctor twice, but it's still not better.
6   We .... why Sara is upset, but she .... to us for ages.
7   Why .... you .... at me? I suppose you
    .... a woman on a motorbike before!

18 Complete the sentences with suitable verbs. Use the present perfect simple or continuous or the present simple or continuous.

1 I've been photocopying the reports all morning, but I still haven't finished.
2 I don't want to spend a lot of money today because I ....
   as much as I can until I .... on holiday.
3 I remember meeting your brother last summer, but I ....
   him this year. What .... since then?
4 I .... with my cousin in London. I ....
   there before, but he .... there for several years, so he can
   show me around.
5 I'm sorry I'm late. .... a long time?
6 Why .... for a little while? You ....
   a break since we started work.
7 We .... this stupid film since lunchtime. Let's switch
   over to the other channel.
8 Jenny's really excited about going to Spain. She ....
   there before, although she .... Spanish for several years.
9 Peter rarely .... time to visit his parents these days, but he
   .... lunch with them tomorrow because it's his father's birthday.

19 Fill the gaps in this letter with suitable verbs. Use the present perfect continuous or simple, or the present continuous or simple.

> Dear Francesca,
>
> We (1) **are having** a wonderful time here in York. We (2) ....
> here for three days now and we (3) .... to stay for the rest
> of the week because we (4) .... ourselves so much. We
> (5) .... the Cathedral and the Castle Museum and this
> morning we (6) .... around the little old-fashioned streets,
> looking at the shops and cafés. I'm writing this while we stop for a cold drink
> before lunch. We (7) .... much money yet but we'll get
> some souvenirs before we leave. Besides the sightseeing, we (8) ....
> some exercise. The countryside around York is lovely and we (9) ....
> .... some lovely long walks. Fortunately, the weather (10) ....
> .... very good so far. People (11) .... it can be very
> cold and it often (12) .... for days! As this is the first time I
> (13) .... to England. I (14) .... I'm just
> lucky.
>
> See you soon,
> Roberta

20 *Read the conversation below and fill the spaces with a verb in a suitable tense.*

Brian and Jessica are on a training course at a company that publishes popular magazines.
During their first morning, they meet for a coffee.

BRIAN: Well, Jess, what have you been doing this morning?

JESS: Oh, it's been really busy. I (1) **'ve been going** round all the different departments to see what they do. What about you? (2) **Have you seen** anything interesting?

BRIAN: I (3) .... to the finance department, accounts and personnel.

JESS: That doesn't sound very exciting!

BRIAN: No, you're right. But this afternoon I'm going to see the art department, where they (4) .... the designs for all the magazines.

JESS: Yes, I (5) .... that department already. They (6) .... some fascinating pictures today, but they don't always have such interesting material, they said. And the editors (7) .... always .... things at the last moment, which (8) .... everyone very irritable.

BRIAN: And I hear that the art editor has a very short temper.

JESS: Don't worry, he's not there today. He (9) .... to some exhibition.

BRIAN: Oh, good. Hey, who's that man over there? He (10) .... us since we came in.

JESS: The one by the door? I don't know. He (11) .... like a lawyer or something, not a journalist. Perhaps he (12) .... only .... here to look round, like us.

BRIAN: Careful, he (13) .... this way.

MAN: Excuse me, are you the two trainees who (14) .... the day here?

JESS: That's right.

MAN: (15) .... yourselves?

BRIAN: Er, yes. Thank you. But –

MAN: Oh, yes. I'm David Gordon. I (16) .... this company.

Present perfect, present and past
(*I have done / I have been doing, I do / I am doing* and *I did*)

21

A   *Read this application letter. There are 7 grammar mistakes in it. Find and correct them.*

> Dear Mr Aziz,
>   I would like to apply for the job of shop manager which I see advertised in the local paper.
>   I am twenty years old. I was born in France but my family moved to England when I was twelve and I am living here ever since. I have left school for three years and since then I am having several jobs in shops. For the past six months I am working in Halls department store. The manager has been saying that he is willing to give me a reference.
>   I speak French and English fluently and I have learnt German since I left school, so I speak some German too.
>   I hope you will consider my application.
>   Yours sincerely,
>   Louise Brett

B   *Write an application letter for this job. You may write for yourself or you may invent an applicant.*

> Bright, helpful person required to help for two months in souvenir shop this summer. Must speak some English in addition to at least one other language. Experience and qualifications not essential, but desirable. Excellent pay and conditions. Write, giving details, + one referee, to: Ms J. Sparks, 'The Old Shop', High St, Cherley, Yorks.

Present perfect and past simple (*I have done* and *I did*)

22   *Match the two halves of these sentences.*

1 My little brother started school	a	all day.
2 The Prime Minister hasn't been abroad	b	when he was six.
3 I caught a cold	c	in the 19th century.
4 My father has been asleep in bed	d	since January.
5 The Red Cross started	e	several minutes ago.
6 The dentist has asked us to wait	f	when we went out in the rain
7 The last bus left	g	for a few minutes.

23 *Choose the correct form of the verbs.*

1 My sister <u>has been</u> / ~~was~~ interested in medicine ever since she ~~has been~~ / <u>was</u> a child.
2 How long <u>have you studied</u> / <u>did you study</u> before you <u>have qualified</u> / <u>qualified</u>?
3 Where <u>have you first met</u> / <u>did you first meet</u> your husband?
4 Is this the first time <u>you've cooked</u> / <u>you cooked</u> pasta?
5 We <u>have wanted</u> / <u>wanted</u> to go to the theatre last night, but there <u>haven't been</u> / <u>weren't</u> any seats.
6 Oh, dear. What can we do? I'm sure something dreadful <u>has happened</u> / <u>happened</u>; we've <u>been waiting</u> / <u>we waited</u> over an hour and he <u>hasn't phoned</u> / <u>hasn't been phoning</u> yet.
7 We <u>have posted</u> / <u>posted</u> the parcel three weeks ago. If you still <u>haven't received</u> / <u>didn't receive</u> it, please inform us immediately.

24 *Alex wants to go to an art college and is being interviewed by Tom Smith, one of the lecturers. Complete the questions which Tom asks him. Read the whole conversation before you start.*

TOM: Right, Alex, let's find out something about you. You're obviously not a teenager, so when (1) ..**did you leave**... school?
ALEX: Five years ago, actually.
TOM: And where (2) .**have you been**.. since then?
ALEX: Well I've had several jobs.
TOM: What (3) .... first?
ALEX: I worked in a café for about a year. I needed to save some money.
TOM: Why (4) .... money?
ALEX: I wanted to travel a bit before I started studying.
TOM: Where (5).. to go?
ALEX: Well, the Middle East, Latin America, Australia –
TOM: Good Lord! And (6) .... all those places?
ALEX: No, not yet. I've been to Brazil and Peru so far. And I spent some months in Turkey.
TOM: What (7) .... there?
ALEX: I stayed with some friends near Izmir. It was wonderful.
TOM: You're very lucky. And now you want to come to college. (8) .... some pictures to show me?
ALEX: Um, yes, I have a small portfolio here.
TOM: Where (9) .... this work?
ALEX: Mostly in Turkey.
TOM: Why (10) .... any in South America?
ALEX: I didn't have time really. And I was travelling light, I just did some pencil sketches.
TOM: (11) .... them here with you?
ALEX: They're at the back of the portfolio.
TOM: Well, Alex, I'm very impressed. When (12) .... interested in painting and drawing?
ALEX: I think I always have been.
TOM: I can believe that. Will you come with me? I want to show this work to my colleagues right away.
ALEX: Of course. Thank you very much.

25 *Complete the sentences by writing about yourself and some of the subjects in the pictures.*

drive / car	go / swimming	ride / bicycle	study / English	eat / burger
ride / motorbike	do / washing up	go / skiing	suck / thumb	eat / birthday cake
go / windsurfing	get / married	break / leg	pass / exam	go / roller-skating

1 I haven't been swimming. since the spring.
2 Yesterday I drove my car into a wall .
3 In the past six months, I ....
4 I .... yet, but I hope to one day.
5 Since my last birthday, I ....
6 I .... recently.
7 Last year I ....
8 Six months ago I ....
9 I .... in my life.
10 I .... when I was a child.
11 I .... yesterday evening.
12 This week I ....

26 *Fill the gaps in these sentences with a suitable verb. Use either the present perfect or past simple.*

1 Bill .has been... away from work all this week.
2 Glenda .worked extremely... hard when she was a student.
3 Pippa .... rather unfriendly recently.
4 Eric .... the door before I rang the bell.
5 How long .... Neil .... his present job?
6 .... Tina .... her parents since she got married?
7 Why .... you .... your coat on? It's not cold.
8 Jock .... to me about his problems last night.
9 Fred .... his map. We'll have to go back for it.
10 Jane .... more money in her last job, but she enjoys this one more.

27 *Fill the spaces in the conversation with suitable verbs. Use the past simple or present perfect.*

Rosie is talking to Marcus, who has recently come to work in the same company as her.

ROSIE: So, Marcus, are you settling in here OK, do you think?
MARCUS: Oh, yes. Everyone (1) .has been... very friendly. I (2) .expected. to have quite a lot of
          problems, but I (3) .haven't had... any really. Not here at work, anyway.
ROSIE: Do you mean there (4) .... other problems?
MARCUS: Well, I (5) .... to move out of the flat I (6) ....
          .... when I first (7) ....
ROSIE: Oh dear. Why (8) .... you .... to do that? Wasn't it
          comfortable? Our personnel department (9) .... you to find
          it, (10) .... they?
MARCUS: That's right. It was a good flat. I (11) .... living there
          very much. Unfortunately, the journey to work was too long. The bus routes
          changed just before I (12) .... to work here and it
          (13) .... me two hours to get here every day. So I
          (14) .... to a place just round the corner from here.
          Everything's fine now.
ROSIE: I hope all this trouble (15) .... (not) you sorry that you
          came here.
MARCUS: Not at all. I'm really enjoying the work. And I (16) .... a
          lot of new friends already.
ROSIE: That's good. Oh, well. We'd better get on with some work now, I suppose.
MARCUS: I guess so. See you later.
ROSIE: Yes. Bye.

28 *Read the following passage and put the verbs in the correct form, present perfect or past simple.*

Then and now

TWENTY YEARS ago few people (1) ..realised... (realise) that computers were about to become part of our daily lives. This short period of time (2) ...has seen....... (see) enormous changes, in business, education and public administration. Jobs which (3) .... (take) weeks to complete in the past, are now carried out in minutes. Clerks who (4) .... (spend) all day copying and checking calculations are now freed from these tedious tasks. In offices, the soft hum and clicking of word processors (5) .... (replace) the clatter of typewriters. Schoolchildren (6) .... (become) as familiar with hardware and software as their parents (7) .... (be) with pencils and exercise books. Computerisation of public records (8) .... (enable) government departments to analyse the needs of citizens in detail. Some of us may wonder, however, whether life (9) .... (really/improve) as a result of these changes. Many jobs (10) .... (disappear), for example, when intelligent machines (11) .... (take) over the work. Employers complain that clerical staff (12) .... (become) dependent on calculators and cannot do simple arithmetic. There are fears that governments (13) .... (not/do) enough to ensure that personal information held on computers is really kept secret. Certainly, many people may now be wondering whether the spread of computers (14) .... (bring) us as many problems as it (15) .... (solve).

Past simple, past continuous and past perfect
(*I did, I was doing* and *I had done / I had been doing*)

29 *Choose the correct form of the verbs.*

CONFERENCE REPORT

(Parkhouse Hotel   5th September)

The conference was very successful. The seminars and talks
(1) were / had been extremely interesting and it was obvious that all the speakers
(2) had prepared / prepared their material very thoroughly. Everyone agreed that
this should become an annual event.
There were however a number of administrative problems. When we
(3) arrived / had arrived, we (4) discovered / had discovered that the hotel
manager (5) reserved / had reserved the wrong room for us and therefore we
(6) did not have / had not had enough space. Unfortunately, he could not let us
have the larger room because he (7) gave / had given it to another group, even
bigger than ours.
He (8) also misunderstood / had also misunderstood the letter explaining what food
we (9) required / had required. In fact, we (10) suspected / had suspected that he
(11) lost / had lost the letter. We do not recommend using this hotel again.

30 *Most of the sentences have one verb in the wrong tense. Correct them or write* **right**.

1 I was pleased to see my old college friends at the conference last week as we didn't see each other since we finished our course. ....*as we hadn't seen each other* ....

2 We had to wait for hours at the airport because the bad weather had delayed all the flights. .RIGHT....

3 Many modern medicines were not invented by western scientists but by tribal people who had been using them for generations before the Europeans arrived. ....*Right*...........

4 We missed our train, so by the time we reached the theatre, the play ended and the audience was leaving the theatre. ....

5 At the end of their meal they found they couldn't pay the bill because they didn't bring any money with them. ....

6 The children were thrilled when they unwrapped the electronic toys, but when they discovered that nobody bought a battery they were very disappointed. ....

7 When I came out of the cinema I had found that a thief had taken my car radio. ....

8 At first the authorities thought the athlete had been taking drugs, but they soon realised they mixed up the results of the tests. ....

9 When the film star came into the restaurant I didn't recognise her because I didn't see any of her films. ....

10 When we reached the city centre we couldn't find a parking space, so we had decided to go by bus the next time. ....

31 *Complete the following conversation using the verbs supplied.*

Jean has called to see her boyfriend Gary.

GARY: Jean, I'm surprised to see you.

JEAN: Well, I think you owe me an explanation.

GARY: Me? What about you?(1) ..*I saw*.. (I / see) you in the café last night. (2) **We had arranged** (we / arrange) to meet at the cinema, if you remember.

JEAN: So why (3) ..*didn't you come*... (you / not / come) into the café if you saw me?

GARY: (4) .... (I / be) too angry. And cold. (5) .... (I / wait) outside the cinema for three-quarters of an hour.

JEAN: But why? (6) .... (you / not / get) my note?

GARY: What note?

JEAN: The note (7) .... (I / leave) here yesterday afternoon. When (8) .... (I / go) past the cinema yesterday lunchtime (9) .... (I / notice) that (10) .... (they / change) the film. So (11) .... (I / put) a note under your door to tell you.

GARY: (12) .... (I / not / find) any note.

JEAN: It must be here. Let me look. Yes. Oh dear. I'm afraid (13) .... (it / slip) under the mat.

GARY: Oh. I'm sorry I was angry. It's just that, well, while (14) .... (I / wait), I was worried about (15) .... (what / happen) to you. And then, (16) .... (I / see) you in the café. (17) .... (you / laugh) with your friends and (18) .... (I / realise) that (19) .... (you / sit) there quite comfortably with them all evening. (20) .... (I / just / lose) my temper.

JEAN: Never mind. Let's forget it. Where shall we go now?

32 *Using the information given, complete each sentence with a suitable verb. Use the past perfect simple or continuous.*

1 Maggie worked in the garden all afternoon. Then she took a hot bath.
   Maggie took a hot bath because she .had been working.. in the garden all afternoon.

2 Graham went for a walk. In the woods he saw some rare birds. When he got home he wrote a letter to the local newspaper about them.
   Graham wrote to the local newspaper about some rare birds which he .had seen. while he was walking in the woods.

3 Rebecca came top in the final examination. Her father bought her a car as a reward.
   Rebecca's father bought her a car because she .... top in the final exam.

4 Henry came home from work early. He cooked lunch. His family were very impressed.
   Henry's family were very impressed to discover that he ....
   lunch when he came home from work early.

5 Greta worked very hard all morning. Her boss gave her an extra half hour for lunch. She boasted about it.
   Greta boasted that her boss .... her an extra half hour
   for lunch because she .... very hard all morning.

6 Patrick went to the disco. He came home very late. His mother was worried and she told him off when he got in.
   Patrick's mother told him off when he came home late because she ....
   about him all evening.

7 Bruce tried to mend a broken window. He cut his hand. He went to hospital.
   Bruce went to hospital because he .... his hand while he was trying
   to mend a broken window.

8 I lost my watch. We had looked for it for hours. I was very pleased when my son found it.
   I was very pleased when my son found my watch because we ....
   for it for hours.

9 Isobel attended a language course. She made some new friends. She sent postcards to them.
   Isobel sent postcards to the new friends she .... while she was
   attending a language course.

33 *Supply suitable verbs for the following conversation.*

Ann is getting ready to leave her office. A colleague, John, comes into the room.

JOHN: Oh, Ann, I'm glad I've caught you. Can you stay on and help us finish some work? You
   remember the new client I (1) .was telling.. you about yesterday? Well, we've got to do a
   presentation to her tomorrow.

ANN: But I (2) .... just ....

JOHN: You don't have to go, do you, though? You (3) .... your
   shopping at lunchtime, (4) .... (not) you?

ANN: And now I want to go home.

JOHN: Oh, come on Ann, please. It'll only be for an hour.

ANN: That's what you (5) .... last time. I (6) ....
   letters for two hours, then when I (7) .... nearly ....
   them all, you (8) .... me do half of them again because you
   (9) .... (not) me the right address file, so I (10) ....
   ....them all wrong!

JOHN: OK, if that's how you feel about it. But next time you need help, don't be surprised if I
   remind you that you (11) .... to help me!

Past simple, past continuous and used to

(*I did, I was doing,* and *I used to do*)

34 *Choose the correct form of the verbs.*

1 Mary met her husband while she <u>worked / was working / used to work</u> in the States.
2 Why does Warren keep shouting at people? He <u>wasn't / wasn't being / didn't use to be</u> so bad-tempered.
3 How long is it since you <u>had / were having / used to have</u> a holiday?
4 The government <u>provided / were providing / used to provide</u> much more help for disabled people than they do now.
5 It's all very well complaining you haven't any money, but while you were travelling around the world, I <u>studied / was studying / used to study</u> sixteen hours a day for my exams.
6 The only time I ever <u>rode / was riding / used to ride</u> a horse, I <u>fell / was falling / used to fall</u> off in the first five minutes.

35 *In some of these sentences you can use* **used to** (**used to work / used to play / used to be,** *etc.*) *instead of the past simple* (**worked/played/was,** *etc.*). *Where possible rewrite the sentences using* **used to.**

1 Every summer, Eileen stayed with her grandparents while her parents were away on holiday.
  .... *Eileen used to stay with her grandparents* ....
2 Bruce drove the new lorry to Scotland, stopping one night in the north of England.
  ..NO CHANGE..
3 My aunt had a dog which she had rescued from drowning when it was a puppy.
  ....
4 As Mary was getting out of the boat her foot slipped and she fell into the river.
  ....
5 Before the new shopping mall was built, there was a football pitch here for the local children. ....
6 Jasper grumbled that bread didn't taste like cardboard until the supermarkets started making it. ....
7 During our voyage across the Atlantic I took several photos of the great seabirds which followed the ship, riding on currents in the air. ....
8 While I was waiting for the bus I noticed a group of tourists who were listening intently to a guide. ....
9 The punishments at our school were very harsh before the new head teacher was appointed.
  ....
10 As children we spent a lot of time helping with the household chores, but we didn't help in the garden. ....
11 The politicians made innumerable promises before the election, but kept none of them, as usual. ....

36 *Choose the correct form of the verbs.*

It is sometimes said that there is nothing new in the world of fashion. Annabelle was a well-known model during the seventies. When her children were in their early teens they (1) <u>were enjoying / used to enjoy</u> looking at her old photo albums. They (2) <u>were finding / found</u> it hard to believe that she (3) <u>was wearing / used to wear</u> such strange clothes. (4) <u>Did people really use to think / Were people really thinking</u> flared trousers looked good? And those ugly platform shoes! She (5) <u>was admitting / admitted</u> that people (6) <u>were often falling / often used to fall</u> over because the heels were so high. In the early nineties, however, Annabelle noticed to her amusement that seventies styles (7) <u>were / used to be</u> in fashion again. 'I (8) <u>planned / was planning to</u> throw all my old clothes away,' she said, 'but my daughter went to a party last week, and guess what she (9) <u>used to wear / was wearing</u> – that's right, some of my old clothes!'

37 *Write a sentence for each of the following using* **used to** *or* **didn't use to**.

1 I had a lot of money but I lost it all when my business failed. ..I used to be rich...

2 I quite like classical music now, although I wasn't keen on it when I was younger.

....

3 I seem to have lost interest in my work.

....

4 My sister can't borrow my jeans any more, she's put on so much weight.

....

5 I don't mind air travel now that I can afford First Class.

....

6 My brother had his hair cut short when he left college.

....

7 I gave up smoking five years ago.

....

8 My parents lived in the USA when I was a child.

....

9 When he was younger, my uncle was a national swimming champion.

....

10 Since we've lived in the countryside, we've been much happier.

....

38 *Write true sentences about yourself, using* **used to** *or* **didn't use to** *and one of the words in the box.*

holidays	television	cinema	homework	jeans
friends	restaurant	music	lipstick	grandparents

1 I used to go on holiday with my parents, but now I go with my friends.
2 I didn't use to wear jeans when I was a child.
3 ....
4 ....
5 ....
6 ....
7 ....
8 ....

Present, present perfect and past

Units 1–18

39 *Choose the correct form of the verbs. Read through each conversation before you start.*

A TERRY: What (1) <u>did you do</u> / ~~have you done~~ / ~~had you done~~ last night?
   ANGIE: Well, I (2) <u>have hoped / have been hoping / had been hoping</u> to go out, but I
      (3) <u>have had / had / had had</u> too much work.

B PETE: What part of Birmingham (4) <u>do you live / did you live / have you lived</u> in when you
      (5) <u>were / have been / were being</u> a student?
   PATRICK: A place called Selly Oak. (6) <u>Do you know / Did you know / Have you known</u> it?
   PETE: Oh, yes. I (7) <u>was passing / used to pass / have passed</u> through it nearly every day when
      I (8) <u>was living / have been living / have lived</u> there.

C GILLIAN: (9) <u>Do you write / Have you written / Were you writing</u> to the bank manager yet?
   MARK: I (10) <u>haven't finished / hadn't finished / didn't finish</u> yet. (11) <u>I've been trying / I've tried
      / I tried</u> to decide what to say.
   GILLIAN: Hurry up! He (12) <u>is expecting / has expected / has been expecting</u> your reply since last
      week.

D BRIAN: Our teacher (13) <u>invites / has invited / invited</u> the class to his house on Saturday.
      (14) <u>Do you go / Are you going / Have you gone</u>?
   LUKE: I'm afraid not. I (15) <u>work / used to work / am working</u> for my father on Saturdays.

E PHILIPPA: When (16) <u>did you hear / have you heard / had you heard</u> your exam results?
   CLARA: When I (17) <u>had phoned / phoned / have phoned</u> my teacher. She (18) <u>has been checking /
      has checked / was checking</u> the list when I (19) <u>had rung / rang / am ringing</u>, so she
      (20) <u>was telling / told / tells</u> me then.
   PHILIPPA: (21) <u>Have you expected / Have you been expecting / Had you been expecting</u> to do so
      well?
   CLARA: Not really, to be honest!

40 *Complete the sentences using the verbs given.*

1 Tom has had to give up playing football since he ..broke.. (break) his ankle.
2 Where ..are you going.. (go) for your holiday next year?
3 How often .... (visit) your cousins when you
.... (be) in the States last year?
4 I .... (not / pay) for my ticket yet. How much
.... (owe) you?
5 The hotel manager called the police when he .... (discover) that a
guest .... (leave) without paying his bill.
6 I don't know what .... (happen) to Sharon. She ....
(be) such a hard worker, but now she .... (lose) interest in everything.
7 We .... (have) a fire in the office last week. Everything
.... (go) very well up till then, but we ....
(sort) out the mess ever since, as you can imagine.
8 My grandmother was a wonderful woman. She .... (spend) most of
her life teaching adults who .... (miss) the opportunity to go to
school when they .... (be) children and ....
(never / learn) to read.
9 I .... (always / want) to visit Japan, and now I
.... (have) the chance, I .... (decide) to take it.

Present tenses for the future and will/shall
(*I do, I am doing* and *I'll do*)

41 *Choose the correct form of the verbs.*

A BEN: Are you busy this week, Sam?
   SAM: Not particularly. (1) <u>I revise / I'm revising</u> until Wednesday because I've got an exam,
         but (2) <u>that only lasts / that is only lasting</u> until midday and then I'm free.

B PAT: Oh dear, I've spilt my coffee.
   ALAN: (3) <u>I get / I'll get</u> a cloth.

C WILL: What time (4) <u>does your evening class finish / is your evening class finishing</u>?
   LIZ: Half past nine.
   WILL: (5) <u>Shall I come / Do I come</u> and collect you?
   LIZ: Thanks, but (6) <u>I meet / I'm meeting</u> my sister for a drink.

D MIKE: Mum, (7) <u>will you talk / are you talking</u> to Dad for me?
   MUM: What's the problem?
   MIKE: Last week he said I could use the car at the weekend but now (8) <u>he doesn't let / he
         won't let</u> me after all. I need it to get to the match (9) <u>I play / I'm playing</u> on Sunday.
   MUM: OK. (10) <u>I try / I'll try</u> to make him change his mind. I expect (11) <u>he's agreeing / he'll
         agree</u> when I explain.

E VALERIE: How soon (12) <u>are you / will you be</u> ready to leave?
   SOPHIE: Oh I can't go out until (13) <u>it will stop raining / it stops raining</u>. I haven't got a coat.
   VALERIE: OK. I don't think (14) <u>it goes / it will go</u> on for long. (15) <u>I tidy / I'll tidy</u> my desk while
         (16) <u>we're waiting / we wait</u>.

42   *Complete the following conversation by expanding the sentences as shown.*

Greg is talking to his personal assistant, Brian, about a business trip he is taking tomorrow.

GREG: Have you completed the arrangements for my trip yet, Brian?
BRIAN: Well, I've made the reservations, but there are still some details to confirm.
(1) **Your plane leaves** (Your plane / leave) at eight-thirty, so (2)
.... (I / collect) you from your house at six.
GREG: Six! (3) .... (I / have to) get up in the middle of the night.
BRIAN: I'm sorry, it's unavoidable. You have to check in by seven and I think
(4) .... (there / probably / be) a long queue.
GREG: Oh, very well. What about my meetings?
BRIAN: First, (5) .... (the Managing Director / come) to the airport to
meet you.
GREG: Good. (6) .... (we / be) able to talk on the way to the factory.
BRIAN: (7) .... (the conference / not / open) until noon.
(8) .... (I / make sure) you have a programme before you leave.
GREG: Thank you. (9) .... (I / read) it on the plane, I expect. Now, let's
get on with some of today's work!
BRIAN: By all means.

43   *Complete the following five sentences about yourself, using the words given.*

1 This lesson .**ends at twelve o'clock.**. (end)
2 At the weekend .**I'll probably go to the cinema.**. (probably go)
3 Next summer .... (visit)
4 When I finish this exercise, ... (be)
5 Tomorrow evening I expect .... (eat)
6 At the end of my course .... (probably speak)
7 My next class .... (begin)
8 Next week .... (have)
9 My course .... (finish)

44   *Imagine that you are in the following situations. Write what you say, using* **will**, **shall** *or* **won't**.

1

YOU

You offer to help her.
I'll take the briefcase for you.. *or*
Shall I carry something?

2

Don't be late.

YOU

You promise not to be late.
....
....

→

3

You agree to deliver the goods on Friday.

....

....

4

You make a suggestion.

....

....

5

You ask them to stop fighting.

....

....

6

You explain the problem with the door.

....

....

7

You offer to phone for an ambulance.

....

....

8

You refuse to pay until you've checked that your goods aren't damaged.

....

....

The future: will/shall, going to and present continuous
(*I'll do, I'm going to do* and *I'm doing*)

45 *Choose the correct form of the verbs.*

1 Oh no! Look at the time! <u>I'll be / I'm going to be</u> terribly late.
2 If you want to go to the shop, you can borrow my brother's bicycle. I'm sure <u>he won't mind / he's not going to mind</u>.
3 <u>I'll go / I'm going to go</u> into town this afternoon. Can I get you anything?
4 <u>Will you hold / Are you going to hold</u> this box for a moment while I unpack it?
5 I hear the government has announced <u>they'll raise / they're going to raise</u> taxes again.
6 <u>My car won't start / My car isn't going to start</u>. It must be the cold, I think.
7 <u>I'll start / I'm going to start</u> a new job next week.
8 I'm so sorry I forgot your birthday. Why don't you come round tomorrow and <u>I'll cook / I'm going to cook</u> you a meal?

46 *Put in the correct form of the verb.*

A ANN: Are you two going out?
   BILL: Yes, why?
   ANN: It just said on the radio that (1) ..it's going to snow... (it / snow).
   BILL: Oh, did it? I (2) ..'ll take.. (I / take) my big coat then.
   JOE: Good idea. So (3) ..will I.... (I).

B COLIN: We've run out of biscuits.
   DAVE: Yeah, I know. (4) .... (I / get) some this afternoon. I've got them on my list.

C ED: Jenny's had her baby.
   GAIL: Really? That's wonderful! (5) .... (I / send) her some flowers.
   ED: (6) .... (I / visit) her this afternoon. (7) ....
         (I / give) them to her for you if you want.
   GAIL: (8) .... (you)? Thanks very much. In that case,
         (9) .... (I / go) and buy them right away.

D IAN: *Casablanca* is on at the Arts Cinema this week.
   JILL: Yes. (10) .... (I / see) it with Roger.
   IAN: Oh.

E KEN: I haven't got a clean shirt. (11) .... (you / wash) one for me?
   LILY: No, (12) .... (I / not). You can do your own washing.

47　Complete the conversations using the verbs given.

Mary and Nigel run a shop together.

Monday
MARY:　I don't know what (1) ..we're going to do.. (we / do). We've hardly made any money for ages.

NIGEL:　I think we should advertise. We can send out leaflets.

MARY:　Yes. (2) ..That will probably get.. (that / probably / get) our name more widely known. But do you think (3) .... (people / come) into the shop?

NIGEL:　Well, we could try advertising in the local paper.

MARY:　That might be better. (4) .... (I / phone) and find out their rates. And what about local radio?

NIGEL:　Good idea. (5) .... (I / phone) them?

MARY:　OK, thanks.

Tuesday
MARY:　We haven't got enough money to pay for all the advertising we need. I've been in touch with the bank. (6) .... (I / see) the manager on Friday.

NIGEL:　(7) .... (he / give) us a loan, do you think?

MARY:　I hope so.

Friday *At the bank*
MANAGER:　So you want to borrow some money. How do want to spend it?

MARY:　(8) .... (we / advertise) on local radio and in the paper. We've planned it carefully. We only need £500.

MANAGER:　Very well. (9) .... (the bank / lend) you the money. But you must pay us back in three months. Can you do that?

MARY:　(10) .... (we / do) it, I promise.

MANAGER:　Now, go and see the loans clerk and (11) .... (he / help) you fill in the necessary forms.

MARY:　Thank you for your help.

MANAGER:　You're welcome.

48　Read the situations and write what you would say in each case. Use **will/shall**, **going to** or *the present continuous. There may be more than one correct answer for some situations, but remember that **going to** is usually used for actions that have already been decided on.*

1　You make your friend a cup of sweet coffee, then she tells you she doesn't take sugar. Offer to make her another one. ..I'm sorry, I'll make you another one...

2　A colleague asks you why you've brought your sports kit to the office. Explain that you have arranged to play tennis after work.
....

3　A friend asks about your holiday plans. Tell her that you've decided not to go abroad this year. ....

4　Your brother lent you some money last week. Promise to pay him back at the weekend.
....

5　A friend is telling you about her wedding plans. Ask her where they plan to go for their honeymoon. ....?

6　Your sister has bought some very cheap CDs. You want to get some too and you've asked her several times where she got them, but she refuses to tell you. Ask why she refuses to tell you. ....?

7 Some friends have asked you to have lunch with them and then go to see a film. Agree to have lunch but refuse to go to the film because you've already seen it.

....

8 You failed an exam last year. Since then you've been working hard. Tell your teacher it's because you're determined not to fail again.

....

9 Your neighbour is playing loud music late at night. You get angry and ask him to turn the volume down.

....?

10 You've been offered the starring role in a Hollywood film and have accepted. Tell your friends about it.

....!

The future: revision

49   *Complete the following conversations by putting the verbs in the right tense.*

A Mick is watching television when his sister Vanessa comes into the room.

MICK: What are you doing in your dressing-gown? It's only eight o'clock.
VANESSA: I don't feel very well. (1) .I'm going to have.. (I / have) an early night.
MICK: Oh, dear. I hope (2) .you feel... (you / feel) better in the morning.
VANESSA: So do I. (3) .... (I / meet) my new boss at ten o'clock.
MICK: I think (4) .... (I / make) some tea when the news
              (5) .... (finish). (6) .... (I / bring) you a
              cup?
VANESSA: No, don't bother. (7) .... (I / try) and go straight to sleep.
              Thanks anyway.
MICK: OK. Sleep well.

B Sandy and Alison are students who have been sharing a flat. Sandy is leaving to do a course abroad.

SANDY: It's hard saying goodbye after so long.
ALISON: We must keep in touch. (8) .... (you / remember) to send me
            your address when (9) .... (you / get) to the States?
SANDY: Of course. (10) .... (I / probably / not / have) time next week,
            because (11) .... (my course / start) the day after
            (12) .... (I / arrive), and (13) .... (I /
            spend) the weekend with some old friends of my father's.
ALISON: Well, you can phone.
SANDY: Yes, I guess so. Do you know what (14) .... (you / do) this time
            next Sunday?
ALISON: (15) .... (I / get) ready to go to London.
SANDY: OK. So, (16) .... (I / phone) about three o'clock next Sunday.
ALISON: Great. (17) .... (I / wait) for your call.

→

C Rebecca and Arnold are leaving the office where they work.

ARNOLD: Would you like to come to a film this weekend?
REBECCA: I'd like to, but I'm afraid (18) .... (I / not / have) time.
ARNOLD: Why? (19) .... (what / do)?
REBECCA: Well, (20) .... (my father / arrive) back from Australia. He's
          been there for six months and (21) .... (we / have) a big party
          to celebrate.
ARNOLD: (22) .... (he / not / be) too tired for a party after his flight?
REBECCA: Yes, and no doubt (23) .... (he / suffer) from jetlag. So, on
          Saturday he can take it easy. But on Sunday, (24) .... (all the
          family / come) for a big barbecue. (25) .... (I / prepare) things
          all day on Saturday.
ARNOLD: What a lot of work for you.
REBECCA: I don't mind. My sisters are very helpful and we're well organised. In fact,
          (26) .... (I / see) someone about hiring a band this afternoon.
          So, I must go now or (27) .... (I / not / get) to their office before
          (28) .... (they / close).
ARNOLD: I hope (29) .... (everything / go) well for you.
REBECCA: I'm sure (30) .... (it / be) a great day. Provided
          (31) .... (the sun / shine), that is!

Can, could and (be) able to   **Units 26 and 27**

50 *Choose the correct form of the verbs.*

1 Why did you walk all the way from the station? You <u>could phone / could have phoned</u> for a lift.
2 I loved staying with my grandparents when I was a child. They let me read all the books in the house and told me I <u>could / was able to</u> go to bed as late as I wanted.
3 This carpet was priced at £500, but I <u>could / was able to</u> get a discount because of this little mark in the corner.
4 I <u>couldn't have found / haven't been able to find</u> my diary for days. It's terribly inconvenient.
5 As soon as she opened the door I <u>could / was able to</u> see from her face that something terrible had happened.
6 I've no idea where my brother is living now. He <u>can / could</u> be at the North Pole for all I know.
7 It's difficult to understand how explorers survive the conditions they encounter in the Antarctic. I'm sure I <u>can't / couldn't</u>.
8 Why did I listen to you? I <u>can be / could have been</u> at home by now instead of sitting here in the cold.
9 The day started off misty, but by the time we had reached the mountain the sun had appeared and we <u>could / were able to</u> climb it quite quickly.

51

Last summer Jack broke his leg. However he still enjoyed himself, even though he didn't join in everything his family did. Look at the pictures and write sentences using **could(n't)** *and* **was(n't) able to.** *Usually you can use both. When can't you?*

1

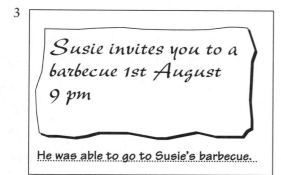

He couldn't swim. / He wasn't able to swim.

2

He could read. / He was able to read.

3

Susie invites you to a barbecue 1st August 9 pm

He was able to go to Susie's barbecue.

4

....
....

5

....
....

6

CONCERT AT CITY HALL JUNE 16th 8PM

....
....

7

....
....

8

WHY NOT ENTER OUR TABLE TENNIS TOURNAMENT SAT 6th AUG

....
....

May/might

52   *Answer the following questions with suitable suggestions, using **may** (or **might**) and the words in brackets.*

1 TERRY: Why is John wearing sunglasses? It's not sunny.
    YOU: (have some problem with his eyes) .He may have some problem with his eyes...

2 JILL: Why didn't Jane come to the party last night?
    YOU: (have a row with her boyfriend) .She might have had a row with her boyfriend...

3 SUE: Why is Alan in such a bad mood today?
    YOU: (sleep badly last night) ....

4 ROY: Why is Shelley looking under the desk?
    YOU: (drop something) ....

5 JILL: Where can I have put my bag?
    YOU: (be under the bed) ....

6 ZOE: Why hasn't anybody said 'Happy Birthday' to me?
    YOU: (plan a surprise) ....

7 TIM: Why does Henry look so miserable?
    YOU: (have some bad news) ....

8 ELLA: Why isn't Sophie in the office today?
    YOU: (work at home) ....

9 JOHN: Why didn't Rosemary come to the cinema last night?
    YOU: (feel tired) ....

53   *Look at these pieces of advice and complete the sentences explaining why the advice should be followed. Use **may** or **might**.*

1 You should reserve a seat on the train when you travel on bank holidays.
If you don't, .you may have to stand up for the whole journey...

2 You'd better not carry that heavy suitcase.
If you do, .you might injure your back...

3 You should carry a map when you visit London.
If you don't, ...

4 You should check the timetable before you leave for the station.
If you don't, ...

5 You ought not to eat too many cream cakes.
If you do, ...

6 You'd better invite your grandmother to your wedding.
If you don't, ...

7 You should have your car serviced regularly.
If you don't, ...

8 You shouldn't go to a party the night before your exam.
If you do, ...

9 You ought to arrive punctually for work.
If you don't, ...

10 You should eat plenty of fresh fruit and vegetables.
If you don't, ...

Must/can't/may/might

54 *Choose the correct form of the verbs.*

1 You <u>must be / can't be</u> very proud of your son winning so many prizes.
2 We thought our cousins would visit us when they were in town last week, but they didn't even phone. I suppose they <u>must be / must have been</u> too busy.
3 The film has been such a big success I guess it <u>must be / can't be</u> easy to get tickets to see it.
4 I'm sure you could mend this if you really tried. You <u>must be / can't be</u> using the right tools.
5 I've just rung the garage to check whether they've fixed my car, but I can't get an answer. I suppose they <u>may have / may be having</u> a tea-break out in the yard.
6 I don't know why you wanted to stay at that party. You <u>might have enjoyed / can't have enjoyed</u> talking to all those boring people.
7 I can't go out this morning. We're getting a new sofa and the store <u>may be delivering / must be delivering</u> it today.
8 You'll have to check these figures again. They're not accurate. You <u>might have been concentrating / can't have been concentrating</u> when you added them up.
9 You <u>must be / must have been</u> thirsty after carrying those heavy boxes. Shall I make some tea?

55 *Complete the conversations with suitable verbs.*

1 JUAN: Maria says her father's a farmer.
  PAUL: But he can't ..be..! They live in the middle of Madrid.
2 JANE: Oh, no. This carrier bag's split.
  KATE: You must ..have put.. too much in it. They're not very strong, you know.
3 MARK: Nigel says he met your sister in Berlin.
  AMY: But he can't .... her there! She's never been to Germany.
4 JIM: Where can I find out about visas for the US?
  JOE: Pia might .... about that sort of thing. She used to work in a travel agency.
5 GARY: This letter says you owe the bank £5,000.
  PHILIP: It must .... a mistake. I don't even have a bank account.
6 SUE: Shall we go to the concert?
  BETH: I'd like to, but you'd better phone first. They may .... all the tickets.
7 BERT: Do you know where my address book is?
  MAY: It could .... in the hall cupboard. I think I saw it there the other day.
8 DAVE: Why didn't Sally come to work in her car today?
  TONY: She didn't say. She could .... it to her sister, I suppose.

56   *Complete the answers to the following questions.* Use **must**, **can't** *or* **might** *with any other words you need.*

1   TONY: Can that be James phoning at this hour? It's gone midnight!
    YOU: It ..might be him.. He said he'd phone if he passed his exam.
2   SALLY: Who's that going into the shop?
    YOU: It ..must be the cleaners.. They always do the floors before we open.
3   BILL: Is that your sister's fur coat?
    YOU: It .... She never wears real fur.
4   CLIVE: I can't remember where I put my briefcase.
    YOU: It .... You often leave it there.
5   DINA: Where did Adam get that new guitar? He hasn't got any money.
    YOU: It .... After all, it was his birthday last
            week.
6   EDDY: Why did Moira ignore me at the party last night.
    YOU: She .... She wasn't wearing her glasses.
7   FRED: Do you think Cindy told the boss I left work early yesterday?
    YOU: She .... She left early yesterday too.
8   HEIDI: Who was that man leaving the library? It looked like Peter.
    YOU: It .... They are so alike that people
            sometimes mistake them for one another.
    HEIDI: Are you sure? I really thought it was Peter.
    YOU: It .... He's in hospital.

57   *Match the two halves of these sentences.*

1 You can't have lived in Tunisia for ten years   a after all your hard work.
2 You must know Tokyo is expensive   b after touring the world for years.
3 You must have met some fascinating people   c if you've lived there.
4 You can't be tired   d without learning some Arabic.
5 You must be exhausted   e when you've just had a holiday.
6 You may find it difficult to settle down   f during your trip to Africa.

58   *Write a sentence for each of these situations using* **must/can't/may/might** (have).

1   Yesterday was payday. I don't believe you're short of money already.
    .You can't have spent all your pay already..
2   It was Linda's suggestion to go for a meal. Surely she doesn't think I'm going to pay for it all?
    She .can't think I'm going to pay for it all..
3   George has been engaged to Kay for three months. Today he received a box with the
    engagement ring in it and all his letters to her.
    Kay ....
4   When Tina got back home, she couldn't find her purse. Perhaps a pickpocket stole it.
    A pickpocket ....
5   Isobel said she was short of money, but she's just moved into a new flat! Her uncle owns
    property in this area.
    She ....

6 This parcel is making a ticking noise – throw it out of the window! I'm sure it's a bomb.
It ....!

7 I don't know who would send me an alarm clock for a present. My brother sometimes plays practical jokes on people, so perhaps it's from him.
It ....

8 Anna's always such a punctual person. The meeting started half an hour ago but she's not here. I know the traffic's very bad this morning.
She ....

Must(n't) / needn't / should(n't) / don't have to

59   *Choose the correct form of the verbs.*

A   JOHN: Can you help me with these letters?
   IRIS: (1) <u>Must we do / Should we do</u> them now? Can't they wait until the morning?
   JOHN: No. I (2) <u>must have posted / should have posted</u> them this morning, really.
   IRIS: Oh, all right then.

B   KEN: Where's Sally? She (3) <u>must be / should be</u> here by now.
   JO: I don't know what's happened to her. She (4) <u>must have missed / should have missed</u> the train.

C   MARY: Happy birthday. I've brought you a present.
   NEIL: Oh, you (5) <u>needn't bother / needn't have bothered.</u>
   MARY: That's OK.
   NEIL: Well, thanks very much.

D   PETER: I'm going to Neil's birthday party this evening. Do you think I (6) <u>must / ought to</u> take him a present?
   RAY: Well, you (7) <u>mustn't / don't have to</u>, I'm sure he doesn't expect one. But personally I don't think you (8) <u>should arrive / must arrive</u> at a party without anything for your host.

E   *At Neil's party*
   NEIL: Why isn't Andrew here? Is he too busy?
   PETER: He told me he hadn't been invited. He's gone away for the weekend.
   NEIL: Oh, dear. His invitation (9) <u>must get lost / must have got lost</u> in the post.

60   *Fill the gaps in the sentences with* **must(n't)**, **needn't** *or* **should(n't)**.

1 We've run out of paperclips. I .... get some more in the morning.
2 You .... finish that report tonight if you're too tired. Midday tomorrow is the deadline.
3 What are you doing here? .... you be at the meeting downtown?
4 He really .... have told his brother about this deal. It was supposed to be absolutely confidential.
5 You .... clean the office because we haven't been using it today, but could you tidy the shelves in the storeroom, please?
6 You .... make so much noise. We'll be asked to leave otherwise.
7 I'm going to be in trouble. I .... have posted these yesterday afternoon and I completely forgot.
8 You .... have typed this – a handwritten note would have been quite adequate.
9 The meeting's finished. We .... find out what's been decided any moment now.

61   *Match the two halves of these sentences.*

1 She should be working   a when she was supposed to be working.
2 She shouldn't stay in bed all day   b because she woke up early anyway.
3 She shouldn't have fallen asleep   c but she's too tired.
4 She mustn't oversleep   d or she'll miss her interview.
5 She doesn't have to get up yet   e unless she's ill.
6 She didn't need to rest   f if she's not going to work today.
7 She needn't have set the alarm clock   g because she wasn't feeling tired.

62   *Complete the second sentence using the correct form of* **must**, **need**, **should** *or* **have to** *without changing the meaning.*

1 It is vital to wear a helmet when you ride a motorbike.
  You *must wear a helmet when you ride a motorbike.*
2 I expect we'll get the contract because we offered the best price.
  We offered the best price so we ....
3 It isn't necessary for us to spend a long time in the museum if it's not interesting.
  We ....
4 It was wrong of you to speak to my mother like that.
  You ....
5 She promised to phone me before lunch. It's seven o'clock now.
  She .... by now.
6 I made far more sandwiches than we needed.
  I .... so many sandwiches.
7 It's essential that my father doesn't find out what I've done.
  My father ....
8 In my opinion it would be wrong for them to move house now.
  I don't think they ....
9 My sister offered me a lift so it wasn't necessary for me to call a taxi.
  As my sister offered me a lift, I ....
10 I suggest it's a good idea to check the timetable before we leave.
  We ....

(Don't) have to / should(n't) / had better (not) / ought (not) to

63 *In some of the following sentences,* **should** *can be replaced by* **had better.** *Which ones are they? Write the new sentence, or write* **no change.**

1 You should always lock the front door when you go out. ..NO CHANGE..
2 I should leave now, or I'll miss my bus. ..I'd better leave now ....
3 I don't think people should keep pets if they don't have time to care for them properly.
....
4 If you want to take photos while we're going round the museum, you should ask permission. We don't want to get into trouble. ....
5 Can you buy me some stamps when you go out? There should be some change in my purse if you haven't got enough money. ....
6 I realise you must be surprised to find us here. Perhaps I should explain what's going on.
....
7 They shouldn't go sailing today. The sea's rough and it might be dangerous.
....
8 People really shouldn't smoke when there are children around. It's such a bad example to them. ....

64 *Anna is giving a colleague some advice about a journey he is planning. Fill the gaps using* **had better, should** *or* **have to.**

ANNA: OK, well, as you haven't done this trip before I
(1) **had better / should**. give you a few tips to save you time
and hassle. First, you (2) .... make
sure you get to the airport really early because you always
(3) .... queue for ages at check-in.
They really (4) .... introduce a more
efficient system, but they won't. Anyway, then you
(5) .... go through passport control
and so on. You (6) .... take
something good to read because you'll have quite a long
wait in the departure lounge. At least you
(7) .... be able to sit down there.
That's another advantage of being early. They
(8) .... provide more seats, in my
opinion. When your flight's called, you (9) ....
follow an official out to your plane.
You (10) .... not take very heavy hand
luggage because you (11) .... carry it
yourself and there aren't any trolleys. Everyone agrees there
(12) .... be, of course, but there
aren't. The flight is quite short. You get a meal, which you
(13) .... eat, even if it's not very
appetising, because you have a long bus journey at the
other end. The hotel is nice. I'm sure you'll like it. Now, do
you have any questions?

65   *Rewrite each of the sentences below beginning as shown. Use* (**don't**) **have to, should** (**not**) *or* **had better** (**not**).

1   It is compulsory to wear a helmet when you ride a motorbike.
    You ..have to wear a helmet when you ride a motorbike....

2   It's advisable to check that all the windows are shut whenever you go out.
    You ....

3   It's not acceptable to borrow money from people you hardly know.
    You ....

4   I suggest we keep the door shut in case someone sees us.
    We ....

5   Regular training sessions are essential if you want to succeed in athletics.
    You ....

6   I don't think it's a good idea to wear that bracelet to school. It might get stolen.
    You ....

7   There is no extra charge for delivery.
    You ....

8   Be sure to pick those tomatoes before they get too ripe.
    You ....

66   *Read about the situations and write sentences with* **ought to / ought not to**. *Some of the sentences are past and some are present.*

1   Andrew is very upset. You shouted angrily at him.
    You ..ought not to have shouted angrily at him...

2   Beatrice is in hospital. Her son hasn't been to see her.
    He ..ought to go and see her...

3   I live in Edinburgh. You went there last week but you didn't visit me.
    You ....

4   Christopher has a new CD player. The children used it without his permission.
    They ....

5   The apple trees have lots of ripe fruit on them but no one can be bothered to pick it so it will
    be wasted.
    Someone ....

6   Darren is five years old. He's playing with a box of matches.
    He ....

7   You've bought a new kitchen gadget. You thought the manufacturers provided an instruction
    leaflet, but you can't find it.
    There ....

8   We called at our friend's house but she was out. We hadn't phoned her before we left home.
    We ....

Should

67 *Complete each of the following sentences twice, once using* **should** *and once using another structure.*

1 After such a hard match, the team captain insisted they ..should take things easy.. *or* ..take things easy.. *or* took things easy...

2 The minister rejected her opponent's demand that she ....
....

3 My doctor explained that it was vital I ....
....

4 Considering that he's always short of money, it's very odd that he ....
....

5 I don't think it'll rain, but you can borrow my raincoat if by any chance it ....
....

6 If you really want to get rich fast, I suggest you ....
....

68 *Fill in the gaps using the words given. There is usually more than one possible answer.*

A BEN: Where's Jack? He promised to check these reports with me.
   SUE: I saw him in the sales office a few minutes ago.
   BEN: It's essential (1) .... (he / see) the reports.
   SUE: Shall I go and look for him?
   BEN: No, (2) .... (I / not / bother). He'll probably turn up in a minute.

B FAY: Are you going to stay in the office over lunchtime?
   JILL: Yes. It's important (3) .... (I / check) these figures. We'll be using them in this afternoon's meeting.
   FAY: Oh, right, yes. Look, (4) .... (Gareth / call), will you say I'm not available until tomorrow? I really haven't got time for him today.

C MICK: I can't find those files anywhere. What (5) .... (I / do)?
   TOM: I really don't know. It's absolutely typical that (6) ....
        (they / disappear) just when you need them. Why don't you ask Rose for a copy of them?
   MICK: I did. She insisted that (7) .... (I / search) for them.
   TOM: She's so unhelpful.

D GAIL: Are you going to buy a house?
   LIZ: Well, the bank's recommendation is that (8) ....
        (we / wait).
   GAIL: Why's that?
   LIZ: They say prices may fall later in the year. They suggest (9) ....
        (we / rent) until the autumn.
   GAIL: I suppose it's only natural (10) .... (they / be) cautious.

69 *Most of the following sentences contain a mistake. Correct them or write* **right**.

1 We were very surprised that Tom behave in such a rude manner. ....

2 I asked a shop assistant for directions and he recommended try the tourist information office. ....

3 The police accepted the recommendation that they reduce the number of officers on duty. ....

4 If I can't leave my bags here, what do you suggest me to do with them? ....

5 I shouldn't go in there if I were you. They're having an argument about money. ....

6 Should I be out when you call, just leave a message with my assistant? ....
....

If I do and If I did

70 *Choose the correct form of the verbs.*

1 If <u>I miss / I'll miss</u> the bus this afternoon, I'll get a taxi instead.
2 We'll have to go without John if he <u>doesn't arrive / won't arrive</u> soon.
3 They <u>won't refund / didn't refund</u> your money if you haven't kept your receipt.
4 Will you send me a postcard when <u>you reach / you'll reach</u> Mexico?
5 If I make some coffee, <u>do you cut / will you cut</u> the cake?
6 <u>Did you work / Would you work</u> harder if you were better paid?
7 If you <u>don't complain / didn't complain</u> so much, you might be more popular.
8 Please don't sign any contracts before <u>I'm checking / I've checked</u> them.
9 <u>Weren't my friends / Wouldn't my friends be</u> envious if they could only see me now!

71 *Fill the gaps in the sentences, using the words given.*

1 If I had more money, ..<u>would you marry</u>.. (you / marry) me?
2 He wouldn't help you if .... (he / not / like) you.
3 .... (you / find) the machine is quite simple to operate if you look at the manual.
4 .... (your parents / not / be) proud if they could see you now?
5 If .... (I / not / revise) thoroughly, I may fail my test.
6 If you wanted to buy someone a really good present, what sort of thing ....
.... (you / look for)?
7 You'd have a lot more friends if .... (you / not / be) so mean.
8 How .... (you / feel) if you were in my position?
9 Would you change your job if .... (you / can)?

72   *Complete the questions in the conversations.*

1   EVA: I don't know what's happened to my dictionary. I've looked everywhere for it.
     SUE: What ..**will you do**.. if ..**you don't find it?**..
     EVA: I suppose I'll have to buy a new one.

2   TIM: I'm thinking of applying for the manager's job.
     ANN: Really? How .... if ....?
     TIM: Oh, about £2,000 a year more than now, I suppose.

3   MAY: I don't know what I'm going to do about money. I can't even pay this week's rent.
     LEE: .... if ....?
     MAY: Well, it would help, of course. But I can't borrow from you.
     LEE: Don't be silly. How much do you want?

4   IAN: This room is so dark and dull.
     PHIL: What .... if ....?
     IAN: White, I think. And I'd have white curtains.
     PHIL: You'd spend a lot of time cleaning it.
     IAN: But at least I'd be able to see!

5   BILL: I don't think I'm going to pass my driving test next week.
     BEN: What .... if ....?
     BILL: I won't be able to get the job I want at the warehouse. They said I must be able to drive.

73   *Lisa is talking to her tutor about what she might do when she leaves college. Use the words given to make sentences.*

TUTOR: Do you have any plans for next year?
LISA: Well, (1) I / travel / if I / afford it. But I don't have any money.
        ..**I'd travel if I could afford it.**..

TUTOR: (2) If you / find / a job abroad / you / take it?
        ....

LISA: (3) If it / be / somewhere I want to go / I / certainly / consider it carefully.
        ....

TUTOR: What about working as an 'au pair'?
LISA: (4) I / only / consider / that if I / be / sure about the family.
        ....

        (5) If they / not / treat / me well, / I / be very miserable.
        ....

TUTOR: Yes. (6) You / have to be sure to use a reputable agency.
        ....

        We have a list in the office. (7) I / get / you one if you / be interested.
        ....

LISA: Yes, I am. Um, (8) if I / decide / to apply / you / give / me a reference?
        ....

TUTOR: Of course. Well, I hope you succeed, whatever you decide to do.
LISA: Thank you very much. I'll let you know.
TUTOR: Yes, I'd like that. Goodbye.
LISA: Goodbye.

74   *Write questions using* **if** *which might produce the following answers.*

1 <u>What would you do if someone gave you a diamond necklace?</u> I'd probably give it to my mother.
2 ....? I'd share it with my friends.
3 ....? I'd call the police.
4 ....? We'd get out as fast as we could.
5 ....? I'd ask my teacher's advice about it.
6 ....? He'd be extremely angry.
7 ....? She'd probably fall over.
8 ....? I'd be late for class.
9 ....? We'd sail around the world.
10 ....? They'd never make any money.
11 ....? There'd be no more wars.

75   *Look at the questions you wrote for 74. Now write your own answers to some of your questions.*

1 What would you do if someone gave you a diamond necklace? <u>I'd sell it and buy a horse.</u>
2 ....
3 ....
4 ....
5 ....
6 ....
7 ....
8 ....
9 ....
10 ....

If I did and If I had done

Units 37, 38 and 39

76   *Match the two halves of these sentences.*

1 If you are promoted	a you'd be able to change the system.
2 If you lost your job	b would you have left the firm?
3 If you were promoted	c you won't be sacked.
4 If you hadn't been promoted	d you won't get a reference.
5 If you had lost your job	e will you make any changes?
6 If you apologise	f you'd regret it.
7 If you are fired	g you'd have lost your car as well.

77   *Complete the following conversations.*

1   SEAN: Why didn't you go to the party last night?
      JIM: I wasn't invited.
     SEAN: So .....would you have gone.... if ..you'd been invited... ?

2   JILL: Jane's a very bright girl, isn't she?
     MILLY: Yes. I .... if ....
               as bright as she is.
     JILL: What would you do instead?
     MILLY: I'd get a job doing something exciting, where I'd meet interesting people and visit lots
               of different places.

3   SAM: Why did you ask Veronica about her boyfriend? It really upset her.
     MICK: Well I didn't realise they'd split up.
     SAM: You didn't know, then?
     MICK: Of course not. If ....

4   TIM: Hey, look at that motorbike. What a beauty.
     PAT: Look out! Mind that litter bin.
     TIM: Ouch! I've hurt my leg.
     PAT: Serves you right. You .... if ....
               ....

5   BEN: Can I have a sandwich?
     JOE: Well, I've only got this one left. No one told me you were going to be here.
     BEN: If ....?
     JOE: Of course I would. Remember to let me know next time.

6   JOHN: Do you love me?
     ROSE: You know I do.
     JOHN: Would ....?
     ROSE: But you're rich.
     JOHN: I've just lost all my money.
     ROSE: You're joking!
     JOHN: Well, yes, I am. But if ....?
     ROSE: I'd say good-bye.
     JOHN: Now you're joking.
     ROSE: Oh no, I'm not!

78 *Read the following letter. For each number, write a sentence, using* **if**. *Write your sentences below the letter.*

Dear Alison,

It was great to hear from you. Thanks for the congratulations and good wishes. I'll pass them on to Charlie when I see him at the weekend. Of course we're very excited about getting married, and frantically busy too, needless to say.

You ask how we met. Well, it's quite a funny story. Do you remember I failed one of my final exams? That meant I had to spend part of the summer in college.(1) And that meant I couldn't go on holiday with my family. The travel company refused to give us a refund because we cancelled too late.(2) I was pretty fed up about it. Then something nice happened. I think the travel agent felt sorry for me, because he had failed his final exam when he was a student.(3) Anyway, he had a cancellation on a tour which started later in the summer. So he was able to transfer my booking.(4) I was really pleased. My father was too, as transferring the booking meant that his money wasn't being wasted.(5) So, I went on this tour. And I met this young man. He was on his own too. He told me his girlfriend should have been with him, but they'd had a row and she'd refused to come.(6) We were the only ones travelling alone, so we found ourselves going round the sights together.(7) He hadn't read about the places we were visiting and I spent most of my time telling him about them.(8) And that was it really. We found we'd fallen in love. Wasn't it lucky I failed that exam? That's how I met my future husband!(9)

Now I must rush off and do some shopping. Will you come and stay soon? It'd be lovely if you could meet Charlie. Write soon. What have you been up to recently?

Lots of love,
Cherry

---

1   If she hadn't failed one of her final exams she wouldn't have had to spend part of the summer
in college.

2   ....

3   ....
....

4   ....
....

5   ....
....

6   ....
....

7   ....
....

8   ....
....

9   ....
....

79 *Look at the pairs of pictures below and imagine yourself in each situation. Write what you would say using* **if**. *There may be several possibilities for each pair.*

1

YESTERDAY

TODAY

If I hadn't dyed my hair my friends wouldn't be laughing at me.

2

YESTERDAY

TODAY

I wouldn't be able to do the test if I hadn't revised thoroughly.

3

TODAY

YESTERDAY

....

....

4

YESTERDAY

TODAY

....

....

5

THIS MORNING   NOW

I haven't got time for breakfast.

I just can't concentrate.

....

....

6

LAST WEEK

I must remember to phone and book seats.

NOW

....

....

7

8 A.M.   9.30 A.M.

You're fired!

Oh damn!

....

....

8

THIS AFTERNOON

Do we need to stop for petrol?

No, we've got more than enough to get home.

NOW

....

....

Conditionals: revision

80 *Complete the following sentences with your own ideas.*

1 What will you do if you .miss your plane..?
2 He'd be more friendly if he .realised who we were....
3 If I hadn't arrived, they .wouldn't have known what to do...
4 If I lend you this book, .will you take great care of it..?
5 You wouldn't have felt ill if you ....
6 If she didn't gossip about her friends, she ....
7 Would you forgive me if I ....?
8 What would happen if I ....?
9 If he had listened to my advice, he ....
10 If you were asked to work overtime, ...?
11 If they ask you for money, ...
12 Would you have sold your car if ....?
13 If you see my brother, ...?
14 They wouldn't mind if we ....
15 She'll soon feel better if she ....
16 If you had been arrested, ...?

Now look at the situations described below. For each one, write a sentence using **if**. *Study the examples carefully.*

17 You should take more exercise because that's the way to get fit.
    If you .take more exercise... you .'ll get fit....
18 Road travel is cheaper than rail travel in this country. As a result we have lots of traffic jams. If road travel .weren't (wasn't) cheaper than rail travel in this country.. we .wouldn't have.... so many traffic jams.
19 Cutting down rainforests has caused many unique plants and animals to become extinct. Many unique plants and animals .wouldn't have become extinct., if people .hadn't cut down rainforests..
20 I can't take much exercise because I don't have enough free time.
    If I .... more free time, I ....
21 Many people didn't realise that smoking was dangerous when they were young. Now they are middle-aged they are having serious health problems.
    If people ...., they .... now they are middle-aged.
22 Hardly anyone was concerned about pollution in the 1960s. The first motorways were built then.
    The first motorways .... if more people .... in the 1960s.
23 The schoolchildren sowed some seeds, but they forgot to water them so they didn't grow.
    The seeds .... if the schoolchildren ....
24 It's important to protect wildlife now or there will be nothing left for future generations.
    If we ...., there .... for future generations.
25 People don't realise how important it is to conserve energy, so they do nothing about it.
    If people .... they .... something about it.
26 Many poor farmers are encouraged to grow crops to sell instead of food. This means they have problems feeding their families when prices fall.
    If poor farmers .... instead of food, they .... feeding their families when prices fall.

I wish ...

81 *Look at the pictures and write what each person wishes, using the words given.*

1

I wish ...

be / tall and strong
<u>I wish I was tall and strong.</u> *or* <u>I wish I</u>
<u>were tall and strong.</u>

2
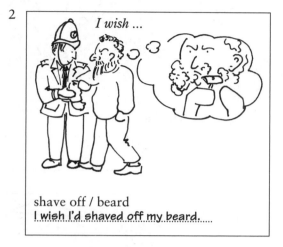

I wish ...

shave off / beard
<u>I wish I'd shaved off my beard.</u>

3

I wish ...

have / car
....
....

4

I wish ...

work / office
....
....

5

I wish ...

live / with my son
....
....

6

HELP!

I wish ...

can / swim
....
....

➜

7

I wish ...

not / listen / hairdresser

....
....

8

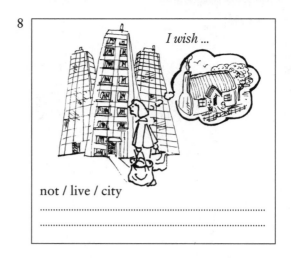

I wish ...

not / live / city

....
....

9

I wish ...

be / helicopter pilot

....
....

10

I wish ...

work / harder

....
....

82 *Bernie and Martin share a room at college. Read what they say about each other, then write sentences beginning* **'I wish he would/wouldn't ...'.**

It's dreadful having to share a room with Bernie. He's so untidy! His books are all over the place, he never washes his coffee cup, he leaves dirty clothes around the room – it's such a mess I can't work. And he comes in late in the evening when I'm trying to sleep and lies in bed watching television. I can't stand it!

Martin

The trouble with Martin is that he never relaxes. He's always working and he's always bad-tempered. He doesn't tell me what's wrong, he just sulks. And he interferes with my possessions. He moves my books around so I can't find them.

Bernie

Martin says   <u>I wish Bernie wouldn't leave his books all over the place.</u>

....

....

....

....

Bernie says   <u>I wish Martin would relax sometimes.</u>

....

....

....

....

83   *Complete the conversations with a sentence using* **wish**.

1   SUE: My mother's really angry with me.
    PAM: Why?
    SUE: Because she found out I left my job.
    PAM: Oh, yes. I told her that.
    SUE: Well, I .<u>wish you hadn't told her</u>.... It's none of your business.
    PAM: I'm sorry.

2   TONY: Have you seen James's new jacket? I bet it was expensive.
    ANA: He told me it cost him £500.
    TONY: I ....
    ANA: Well, you may not be rich, but you're much better looking than James.
    TONY: Am I?

3   GARY: You seem to enjoy dancing with Lionel.
    JANE: Yes, I do. He's a very good dancer.
    GARY: I .... when I was young.
    JANE: You could learn now.
    GARY: Oh, I'd feel stupid in a dancing class at my age.

4   EVA: I went to Norway last month.
    MAY: Really? My brother's living in Oslo now.
    EVA: I .... I could've visited him.
    MAY: Yes, it's a pity. You must tell me if you have to go there again.

5   FRED: My parents moved to New York last month.
    JAN: How do they like it?
    FRED: My mother likes it, but my father misses their old home. He ....
    JAN: Perhaps he'll get used to it.
    FRED: I doubt it.

6   KAY: My brothers are digging a swimming-pool.
    JILL: That sounds like hard work!
    KAY: It is. Actually, I suspect .... But they can't stop
            now. There's a great big hole in the middle of the garden.
    JILL: Yes, I see what you mean.

The passive

84 *Complete the sentences using words from each box.*

| build   paint   design   write   ~~name~~   invent   discover |

| ~~Eric the Red~~   Guglielmo Marconi   the Ancient Egyptians
Crick and Watson   Picasso   George Orwell   Gustave Eiffel |

GREENLAND

1 Greenland ...was named by Eric the Red....
2 *Animal Farm* ....
3 The Pyramids ....
4 The wireless ....
5 *Guernica* ....
6 The Statue of Liberty ....
7 The structure of DNA ....

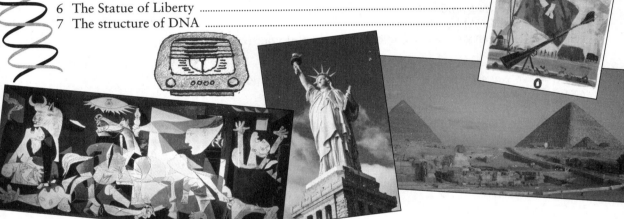

85 *Put the verbs in the present perfect tense, active or passive (**has done** or **has been done**).*

1

(she / open) She's opened it.

2

(the tree / cut down) The tree has been cut down.

56

3

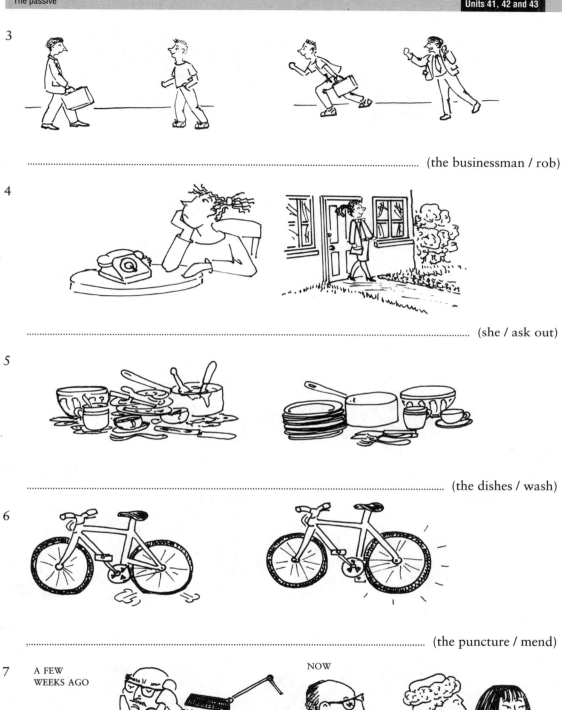

.... (the businessman / rob)

4

.... (she / ask out)

5

.... (the dishes / wash)

6

.... (the puncture / mend)

7   A FEW
      WEEKS AGO   NOW

.... (he / retire)

8

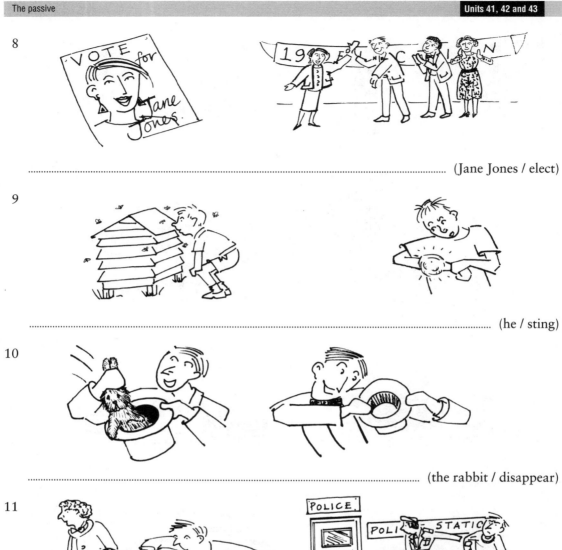

.... (Jane Jones / elect)

9

.... (he / sting)

10

.... (the rabbit / disappear)

11

.... (he / arrest)

12

.... (they / pass)

86   *Rewrite the following newspaper report using passive forms of the verbs underlined.*

DARING RAID AT LOCAL HOTEL

Thieves (1) <u>held</u> the manager of the Ridgeway Hotel at gunpoint last night during a daring raid in which they (2) <u>took</u> nearly £50,000 from the hotel safe. They also (3) <u>broke</u> into several of the bedrooms and (4) <u>removed</u> articles of value.

    The thieves made their escape through the kitchen, where they (5) <u>damaged</u> several pieces of equipment. They (6) <u>injured</u> the chef when he tried to stop them and (7) <u>left</u> him lying unconscious on the floor. Police (8) <u>arrested</u> the thieves early this morning.

1   The manager of the Ridgeway Hotel was held at gunpoint last night.
2 ....
3 ....
4 ....
5 ....
6 and 7 ....
8 ....

87   *Put the verbs in the correct form.*

1 I've collected all the documents that .... (need) for the house sale. Can you take them to the lawyer's office to .... (sign)?
2 Look, this is a secret. Come into the garden where we .... (not / overhear).
3 If you hadn't been so late for work, you .... (sack).
4 This office is very inefficient. The telephone .... (never / answer) promptly, no proper records .... (keep), and, worst of all, no reports .... (written) for weeks.
5 I was so worried about my garden while I was in hospital, but I have very good neighbours. When I got home I could see that the vegetables .... (water) every day and the grass .... (cut) regularly.
6 Can you come to the police station? The man who .... (suspect) of stealing your wallet .... (arrest), and .... (question) at the moment. The police hope he .... (identify), either by you or another witness.
7 We had hoped to see several famous paintings, but the gallery .... (re-organised) at the time of our visit and most of the really valuable works .... (move) for safe keeping.

88 *Most of these sentences contain one mistake. Correct it or write* **right.**

1 My neighbour is very proud of her new grandson who born last week.
....

2 I'm very fond of this old brooch because it was belonged to my grandmother.
....

3 My family live in Scotland but I was educated in France. ....

4 I'm afraid I can't lend you my camera. It's repairing this week. ....

5 The bridge was collapsed during the floods but fortunately no one was using it at the time.
....

6 If you aren't careful what you're doing with that hammer someone will hurt in a minute!
....

7 The word 'stupid' was in my report but it wasn't referred to you. ....

8 I'm sorry I'm late. I got held up in the traffic. ....

9 When did you discover that the money had been disappeared? ....

10 Children under the age of seven do not allow in this pool. ....

89 *Complete the sentences. If possible, use a tense of the verb* **get.** *Otherwise use the verb* **be.**

1 I never found that book we were looking for. It .... lost when we moved
house.

2 After the way he behaved last time he went to their house it's unlikely he ....
asked there again.

3 Naturally this vase is expensive. After all, it .... believed to be over three
hundred years old.

4 I phoned to explain what had happened but I .... cut off before I could finish.

5 There isn't any cheese left; I'm afraid, it .... eaten by the children.

6 He was a well-known expert on animal diseases and his opinions .... greatly
respected.

7 The competition is stiff and she'll be thrilled if her design .... chosen.

8 The book .... torn when the children started fighting over who should read it
first.

9 Please don't touch anything on my desk. You .... employed to answer the
telephone, not to tidy the office.

10 She was quite friendly at first, then she .... promoted and now she doesn't care
about us any more.

90 *Rewrite the sentences beginning in the way shown. Do not use* **by** *unless it is important to the*
meaning.

1 The company has cut all salaries.
All salaries .*have been cut* ....

2 The bank manager kept me waiting for half an hour.
I ....

3 Employers must pay all travel expenses for this training course.
All travel expenses for this training course ....

4 Do you suppose your brother could have written such a letter?
Do you suppose such a letter ....?

5 They use a computer to do that job nowadays.
A computer ....

6 During the recession, the firm was making people redundant almost every week.
During the recession people ....

7 Nobody informed the police that there had been a mistake.
The police ....

8 Where will your company send you next year?
Where will you ....?

9 The news about the famine distressed Josephine.
Josephine ....

10 I've still got the camera because no one has claimed it.
I've still got the camera because it ....

11 Has anyone ever asked you for your opinion?
Have you ....?

12 The children shouldn't have opened that parcel.
That parcel ....

13 All visitors must wear identity badges.
Identity badges ....

91 *Put the verbs into a suitable tense in the passive.*

Mary has just arrived home from work. Neil is already there.

MARY: Hi! I'm back. Sorry I'm late.

NEIL: Hello. What kept you?

MARY: I had to use the ring road and I (1) .... (stick) in a traffic jam for forty minutes.

NEIL: Why didn't you use the usual route?

MARY: Because the road (2) .... (close) until work on the access road to the new hospital (3) .... (complete).

NEIL: When is it due to (4) .... (finish)?

MARY: Well, the access road (5) .... (open) by the Mayor next week, according to the newspaper, and the Health Minister (6) ....
.... (invite) to open the hospital on the same day, but they don't know yet whether she's definitely coming.

NEIL: A lot of money (7) .... (waste) if she doesn't come.

MARY: Why's that?

NEIL: Haven't you seen all those rose bushes that (8) ....
(plant) round the hospital?

MARY: So? They'll be lovely for the patients.

NEIL: But the patients won't be able to see them, because they're round the entrance, and the wards look out in the other direction. A lot of people protested about it, but all their complaints (9) .... (ignore) until it was too late.

MARY: If they had money to spare, it (10) .... (spend) on facilities for patients, not on making the front look pretty for the Minister.

NEIL: Absolutely. It's typical of this local council. They (11) ....
(elect) to save money, but they do just the opposite.

MARY: Perhaps they (12) .... (throw) out at the next election.

NEIL: I hope so. Now, are you ready for supper?

92 Read this letter from Maurice, who is on holiday in Britain, to his sister Sally in New Zealand.
Put the verbs in a suitable tense, active or passive.

> Dear Sally,
>   How are you? We've been having a lovely time. We're being very well looked after
> by our hosts. We (1) .... (take) sightseeing and we
> (2) .... (introduce) to some of their friends, who
> (3) .... (make) us feel very welcome. Last night we
> (4) .... (show) round a castle, by the owner! Most of the
> land in this area (5) .... (belong) to his family for about
> five hundred years. Apparently, the land (6) .... (give) to
> them after one of his ancestors (7) .... (kill) while trying
> to save the king's life. Quite romantic, isn't it?
>   The castle itself was a little bit disappointing, to be absolutely honest. The owner
> told us that it (8) .... (suffer) serious damage during a
> fire about thirty years ago. When it (9) .... (restore) they
> (10) .... (add) central heating and things like that. So
> once you're inside it (11) .... (not feel) much different to
> any other large, old house. But the owner is a real character. He told us lots of stories
> about things that (12) .... (happen) to him when he was
> young. He (13) .... (send) abroad to work in a bank, but
> he hated it, so he (14) .... (behave) very badly in order to
> (15) .... (sack). He kept us laughing for hours. I hope he
> (16) .... (invite) here before we leave.
> I'll have lots more to tell you when we get back. Take care.
>   Yours affectionately,
>   Maurice

93 Complete this conversation with verbs in a suitable tense, active or passive.

Cindy and Petra are members of a volleyball team.

CINDY: Why wasn't Clare at the training session?

PETRA: Haven't you heard? She 's been thrown (1) out for stealing.

CINDY: No! Really?

PETRA: Yes. She (2) .... taking money from someone's bag in the
changing room.

CINDY: Who by?

PETRA: The sports club manager. She (3) .... through the changing room
when she (4) .... Clare with Karen's bag.

CINDY: Oh dear. That's terrible.

PETRA: Clare said she (5) .... to fetch the money by Karen but when
Karen (6) .... about it, she said she (7) ....
(not) what Clare was talking about.

CINDY: But how stupid of Karen to leave money in the changing room!

PETRA: Yes. She (8) .... that by the manager too.

CINDY: She (9) .... (not) it again, anyhow.

PETRA: No, I guess not. What do you think Clare (10) .... now?

CINDY: I don't know. This is the second club she (11) .... to leave, isn't it?

PETRA: Yes. It's hard to know what can (12) .... for someone like Clare.

94 *Look at the pictures and complete the letter explaining why Thomas decided not to stay in Brinmouth for his holiday.*

Dear Vince,

I expect you're surprised I'm not writing from Brinmouth. I went there, but left almost immediately. You remember what a quiet, pretty place it used to be? Well, when I got there, I found it has changed completely.

Some boys (1) ..were riding.. motorbikes along the sand. The inn (2) .has been replaced. by a a new hotel. The station (3) .... The quayside (4) .... as a park for tourist buses. An amusement arcade (5) .... on the park. Children (6) .... video games in the arcade. No one (7) .... sandcastles anymore. A motorway (8) .... over the hill. The sea (9) .... with industrial waste three years ago. No fish (10) .... since then.

Don't you think it's sad?
See you soon,
          Thomas

Have something done

95 *Replace the phrase underlined with the structure* **have something done.**

1 I didn't recognise Sheila. <u>The hairdresser's dyed her hair</u>. *She's had her hair dyed.*
2 I've been getting a lot of annoying phone calls, so <u>the telephone company is going to change my number</u>. ....
3 Gabrielle broke her leg six weeks ago but she's much better now. In fact <u>the doctors should be taking the plaster off</u> tomorrow. ....
4 Since Rowland made a lot of money, he's not content with his little cottage, so <u>an architect's designed him a fine new house</u>. ....
5 This room gets too hot when the sun shines so <u>I'm getting someone to fit blinds on the windows</u>. ....
6 I heard that Mrs Green didn't trust her husband so <u>she hired a detective to follow him</u>!
....
7 We don't really know what Shakespeare looked like. I wish <u>he had asked someone to paint his portrait</u> before he died. ....
8 My sister had always been self-conscious about her nose so she decided to go to a clinic <u>for an operation which will straighten it</u>. ....

Questions

96 *Tony is being interviewed for a job. Look at the interviewer's notes and Tony's answers, then write the questions she is asking Tony.*

1	age?	*How old are you* ?	I'm 18.
2	live locally?	....................?	Yes, I do.
3	address?	....................?	5, Flower Close.
4	when / leave school?	....................?	Last year.
5	which school / go?	....................?	Benham School.
6	work / now?	....................?	Yes, I am.
7	who / work for?	....................?	Millers Limited.
8	how long?	....................?	For six months.
9	enjoy / present job?	....................?	Yes, I do.
10	why / want / leave?	....................?	The pay isn't good.

97 Sonia Schmidt is phoning to book a hotel room. Complete the conversation by putting the words in brackets in the correct order.

RECEPTIONIST: Good morning. Blakeney Hotel.

SONIA: Hello. My name's Schmidt. I'd like to book a room please.

RECEPTIONIST: Certainly. (staying / how many nights / you / be / will?)
(1) *How many nights will you be staying?*

SONIA: Three. Starting next Thursday.

RECEPTIONIST: Yes, we have rooms available. Double or single?

SONIA: Double please. (available / is / one / with a sea view?)
(2) ....?

RECEPTIONIST: Yes. By the way, (have / about / the special offer / we are running / you / at the moment / heard?)
(3) ....?

SONIA: No.

RECEPTIONIST: It's four nights for the price of three. (don't / take / it / advantage / you / why / of)
(4) ....?

SONIA: (have / for it / what / I / to / do / to qualify / do)
(5) ....?

RECEPTIONIST: Just confirm your reservation in writing and pay a ten per cent deposit.

SONIA: (be / much / would / that / how?)
(6) ....?

RECEPTIONIST: £15.

SONIA: Yes. I think I'll do that. (to / make / the cheque / who / I / should / payable?)
(7) ....?

RECEPTIONIST: The Blakeney Hotel.

SONIA: OK. I'll post it today.

RECEPTIONIST: Thank you very much. We'll look forward to seeing you.

SONIA: Thank you. Goodbye.

RECEPTIONIST: Thank you.

98 *Brian has decided to join a Health Club. First, the instructor helps him to plan his fitness programme. Complete their conversation by writing the instructor's questions. You should read the whole conversation before you begin.*

INSTRUCTOR: OK, Brian. Let's find out how fit you are. First of all, (1) <u>how old are you</u>?
BRIAN: I'm thirty-two.
INSTRUCTOR: And (2) ....?
BRIAN: About seventy-five kilos.
INSTRUCTOR: And (3) ....?
BRIAN: One metre eighty.
INSTRUCTOR: (4) ....?
BRIAN: I'm a bus driver.
INSTRUCTOR: Really? So, (5) ....?
BRIAN: Well, I take some exercise, but it's not regular.
INSTRUCTOR: (6) ....?
BRIAN: No, I haven't done any sport since I left school. I just work in the garden and sometimes go for a walk on my day off.
INSTRUCTOR: I see. (7) ....?
BRIAN: Well, yes. I admit I do. Not more than a packet a day, though.
INSTRUCTOR: That's quite a lot, actually.
(8) ....?
BRIAN: I tried once, about a year ago, but I got so impatient I nearly crashed my bus.
INSTRUCTOR: Well, perhaps we can give you some help. It's really important, you know. Come with me and I'll do a few checks and then we'll make a plan for you.
BRIAN: OK. Thanks.

99 *Complete the conversations using the words given.*

1 GRAHAM: Do you know <u>where my football boots are</u>? (football boots)
  ANDREW: In your sports bag, I expect.

2 CUSTOMER: Can you tell me ....?
             (this jacket)
  ASSISTANT: £59.99.

3 ELIZABETH: I'd like to know ....
             (books about Russia)
  LIBRARIAN: They're on the third shelf, beside the window.

4 KENNETH: Do you happen to know .... ?
                  (the last bus)
   MAUREEN: I think it leaves at half past ten.

5 ALEXANDER: Could you explain .... ?
                  (this coffee machine)
   ELEANOR: It's quite simple. You put a coin in here and press the red knob.

6 TERESA: I can't understand ....
                  (the car)
   MARGARET: You've run out of petrol, that's why!

7 RICHARD: Please could you tell me .... ?
                  (the manager's office)
   RECEPTIONIST: It's on the first floor, at the end of the corridor.

8 PHILIPPA: Do you know .... ?
                  (the first Olympic Games)
   WILLIAM: 776 BC.

9 DUNCAN: I can't remember ....
                  (your sister)
   CATHERINE: She was seventeen last March.

100 *Find the mistakes and correct them. If there is no mistake, write* **right**.

1 Have ever you been to Thailand? ....
2 What means this word? ....
3 How much costs it to fly to Australia from here?
   ....
4 We can't remember where did we put our passports.
   ....
5 Had the play already started when you got to the theatre?
   ....
6 Now, come and sit down. Would you like to explain what is the problem?
   ....
7 How long did it you take to get here? ....
8 Now I understand why didn't you tell me about your job!
   ....
9 Excuse me. Can you tell me where the dictionaries are?
   ....
10 Why people in your country don't show more respect to the elderly?
    ....

Reported speech

101 *Last week you had lunch with Rachel, a friend you hadn't seen for a long time. Look at the list of things she said to you, then tell another friend what she said. Use reported speech.*

Rachel

1 I'm going to work in Spain next year.
2 I work for a small publishing company.
3 I'm their marketing manager.
4 The company has opened an office in Barcelona.
5 It's been very successful.
6 I've been chosen to run a new office in Madrid.
7 I'm studying Spanish in the evenings.
8 I don't have much time to enjoy myself.
9 I haven't had lunch with a friend for ages.
10 I hope my friends will come and visit me in Madrid.
11 I went there last week with my secretary.
12 We didn't have much time for sightseeing.
13 I have to get back to work now.

Tell your friend what Rachel said:

YOU

1 Rachel said .....she was going to work in Spain next year......
2 Rachel said ....
3 Rachel said ....
4 Rachel said ....
5 Rachel said ....
6 Rachel said ....
7 Rachel said ....
8 Rachel said ....
9 Rachel said ....
10 Rachel said ....
11 Rachel said ....
12 Rachel said ....
13 Rachel said ....

102   *Last week Julius had flu and had to call the doctor. When he was back at work, he told a colleague about what the doctor said to him. Look at the things his doctor said, then write down what Julius said to his colleague. Change the tense of verbs only where necessary.*

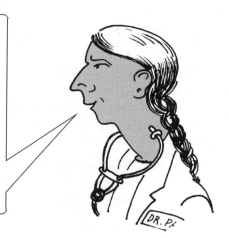

1   You have a high temperature.
2   You don't look after yourself properly.
3   You've obviously been ill for several days.
4   You can't go to work.
5   You're much too thin.
6   You don't eat sensibly.
7   You need to stay in bed.
8   You don't keep your flat warm enough.
9   You've got a nasty cough.
10   You can phone me if you feel worse.
11   You'll feel better in a few days.
12   You need a good holiday.

What did Julius say to his colleague?

1   She said ...I had a high temperature....
2   She said ...I don't look after myself properly.....
3   She said ....
4   She said ....
5   She said ....
6   She said ....
7   She said ....
8   She said ....
9   She said ....
10   She said ....
11   She said ....
12   She said ....

103 *John had a row with his girlfriend, Julie. His friend Mark tried to help them get back together, and talked to Julie for John. Complete the conversation he had later with John.*

MARK: Julie, John's asked me to talk to you.
JULIE: I don't want to speak to him.
MARK: Look Julie, John's really upset.
JULIE: I'm upset, too.
MARK: Will you just let me tell you his side of the story?
JULIE: I'm not interested. He promised to meet me at the restaurant, but he didn't turn up. I don't want to see him again.
MARK: But, Julie, his car had broken down.
JULIE: So? There is a telephone in the restaurant.
MARK: But that's the point. He tried to phone, but he couldn't get through.
JULIE: I don't believe he tried.
MARK: Yes, he did. He came to my flat. Do you believe me?
JULIE: OK. I'll talk to him. Listen, I'm going to be late for work. I'll meet him at six o'clock in the square.
MARK: Thanks, Julie. He'll be really happy. And I promise he'll be there.

JOHN: What did she say?
MARK: She said she (1) .didn't want to talk to you..
JOHN: Well, what did she say when you told her I was really upset?
MARK: She said she (2) .... too, so I asked her to let me tell her your side of the story. She said she (3) .... because you (4) .... at the restaurant, but you (5) .... She said she (6) .... again.
JOHN: Did you explain about the car?
MARK: Yes, and she was very sarcastic. She said there (7) .... at the restaurant. So I told her you couldn't get through, but she said she (8) .... Then I told her you'd been to my flat and asked if she believed me. She said 'OK' and she said (9) .... Then she said she (10) ...., so we had to finish. You have to meet her in the square at six o'clock.
JOHN: Thanks, Mark. I really owe you one.
MARK: That's all right. Just don't be late this evening.

104 You've just arrived at a hotel for a holiday. It's not the same as your travel agent told you it would be. Look at the pictures in your travel agent's brochure and tell the manager what you expected.

IMPERIAL HOTEL

- There's a large swimming pool.
- A disco is held every night.
- You can go horse-riding.
- Room service is available.
- They serve an international menu in the dining-room.
- A fitness centre has been added to the hotel's facilities.
- The tennis courts can be booked free of charge.
- The gardens have a wonderful variety of flowers.
- You'll love the private beach.
- Guests can use the nearby golf course free of charge.

1   The travel agent said there was a swimming pool.
2   He said ....
3   He ....
4   ....
5   ....
6   ....
7   ....
8   ....
9   ....
10   ....

105　Look back at your answers to exercise 96. After his interview Tony told his friends what he had been asked. Check your answers to exercise 96 then write them as reported speech.

1　She asked me ..how old I was...
2　She asked me ....
3　She asked me ....
4　She asked me ....
5　She asked me ....
6　She asked me ....
7　She asked me ....
8　She asked me ....
9　She asked me ....
10　She asked me ....

106　Rewrite the sentences beginning in the way shown.

1　'Where are you going?' asked Tom.
　.Tom asked (me) where I was going...
2　'Where are you going to spend the holiday?' asked Mike.
　Mike asked ....
3　'What will you do when you leave school?' said Jennifer.
　Jennifer asked ....
4　'How did you know my name?' the nurse asked the doctor.
　The nurse wanted to know ....
5　'Do you have an appointment?' said the clerk.
　The clerk asked ....
6　'Have you seen my car keys?' said Bernard to his wife.
　Bernard wondered ....
7　'Why didn't Isobel phone me?' asked her brother.
　Isobel's brother wanted to know ....
8　'Will you carry my briefcase for me please, James?' said Richard.
　Richard asked ....
9　'When can I see the doctor?' Charles asked the receptionist.
　Charles asked ....

107

Anna has just met Colin Boyle, a singer she admires very much. She is telling her boyfriend, Ian, about the meeting, and he wants to know exactly what Colin said to her, and what she said to him.

IAN: Well, what was he like? Was he friendly? What did he say?

ANNA: He was really friendly. (1) <u>He asked me who I was.</u>

IAN: Then what?

ANNA: (2) <u>He asked me where I came from.</u>

IAN: And what did you say?

ANNA: (3) <u>I told him I came from Dublin</u> of course. Then (4) <u>he said that was where he was born too.</u> Then (5) <u>I told him I'd been a fan of his for ages,</u> and (6) <u>he said he was very flattered</u>, and then (7) <u>he asked whether I was going to the concert tonight.</u> So (8) <u>I told him we wanted to but we hadn't been able to get tickets</u>, because they'd sold all but the most expensive ones and we couldn't afford those.

IAN: And did he give you some tickets?

ANNA: No, he didn't. But (9) <u>he did ask the concert hall manager if we could have some at the cheaper price.</u> And the manager said, 'Yes'!

Now write exactly what Anna and Colin said.

1 Colin said: ...<u>Who are you?</u>....

2 Colin said: ....

3 Anna said: ....

4 Colin said: ....

5 Anna said: ....

6 Colin said: ....

7 Colin said: ....

8 Anna said: ....

        ....

9 Colin said: ....

108 Complete the sentences with the correct form of **say** or **tell**.

1 ...Did you tell... your brother the truth about that money?
2 What .... (you) to Wendy last night? She looks terribly upset this morning.
3 Is something wrong? Can you .... me about it?
4 My little sister kept asking me .... her a story but I couldn't think of one.
5 If I asked you to marry me, what .... (you)?
6 I never know what .... to people when they pay me a compliment.
7 Don't worry, I'm sure everything will go smoothly. Anyway, the manager .... to call him if we had any problems.
8 I'll never speak to him again after all the lies he .... me last weekend.
9 If I were you, I .... (not) anything to the police about your suspicions until you have more evidence.
10 Promise you .... (not) anything to my parents. They'll be furious if they find out what I've done.
11 I .... (already) you, I don't know where your diary is.
12 Please .... you'll forgive me. I'm really sorry for all the trouble I've caused.
13 I'm ready to serve the meal. Can you .... the children to go and wash their hands, please?

109 Complete the letter with the correct form of **say** or **tell**.

Dear Stephanie,
I'm writing to (1) ...tell... *you about the discussion I had with my father last weekend. We talked for several hours and I* (2) .... *him all about the plans we've made for our business. At first, he wasn't very interested, he* (3) .... *he didn't think we were old enough to run a business. However, I* (4) .... *him that we had already seen the bank manager, who* (5) .... *that the plan seemed realistic. So then he sat down and asked me* (6) .... *him how much money we'd need to start with, and where we'd sell the stuff we made and so on. Eventually he* (7) .... *to me 'OK, it's a good plan.* (8) .... *Stephanie that I'll lend you some money to get started.' Honestly, I couldn't believe he* (9) .... *it! Isn't it great? I'm really looking forward to seeing you next week so we can talk to him together and get things going.*
All the best,
Neville

110 *Most of the following sentences contain one mistake. Correct it or write* **right**.

1 When I asked Joan about her work she said she had lost her job and is short of money.

   ....

2 Michael explained that he couldn't come to the party because he was working that evening.

   ....

3 We had a great evening with Janet. She was telling about her fascinating trip to Kenya.

   ....

4 I'm sorry to bother you, but you did say to call if I was worried.

   ....

5 We were disappointed when the receptionist told that the hotel was fully booked that week.

   ....

6 The museum guard asked the visitors to not touch the exhibits.

   ....

7 The tour guide explained that the castle is only open on Tuesdays.

   ....

Verb + -ing and verb + to ...

111 *Complete the sentences with the correct form of the verb given. Use* -ing *or* to ...

1 As we don't agree about politics we generally avoid .**discussing**... (discuss) the subject.
2 He doesn't get on with the new boss, so he's asked .**to be transferred**... (transfer) to another branch of the company.
3 Please stop .... (interrupt) me when I'm explaining something to you. You can ask questions at the end.
4 We had arranged .... (meet) in my office so that he could check the documents he needed.
5 I must say, I don't really fancy .... (spend) my whole holiday with your cousins.
6 He admits .... (enter) the house but he says he didn't take anything.
7 I've apologised to her but she still refuses .... (speak) to me.
8 What a dreadful man! Can you imagine .... (live) with him?
9 Of course I'll help you, as long as it doesn't involve .... (lift) anything heavy.
10 Oh no! I've forgotten .... (bring) my briefcase with me. I'll have to go back for it.
11 They had hoped .... (live) in their new house by now, but the builders are still working on it.
12 I don't mind .... (work) late, if it will help at all.
13 I simply can't afford .... (support) you any longer – you'll just have to find a job.
14 We had hoped to finish the project by the end of the month but we keep .... (delay) by changes in the plans.
15 You'd better go and see the boss and say what you've done. If you put off .... (explain) it to her, she'll only be more annoyed.

112 *Complete the conversations.*

A ANN: What are you doing this weekend?
  BILL: I'm hoping (1) *to visit* my parents, if I can.
  ANN: I thought you went to see them last weekend.
  BILL: No, I planned (2) .... them, but they suggested
        (3) .... the visit for a week because they hadn't finished
        (4) .... the spare room.

B CILLA: Can you help me with these packages?
  DAVE: Of course.
  CILLA: I've got to get them all posted today. One of our big customers has said he'll consider
        (5) .... to another supplier if we don't improve our delivery times.
  DAVE: Have we been failing (6) .... on time? I didn't know that.
  CILLA: Apparently someone forgot (7) .... an order last month. So I
        agreed (8) .... them myself this time, because we can't risk
        (9) .... such an important customer.

C JACK: Oh dear, here's another note from Peter.
  SEAN: Why does he keep (10) .... to you?
  JACK: He wants me to join his basketball team. He's offered (11) .... me
        repair my car if I agree (12) .... them. The trouble is, it involves
        (13) .... to a lot of practice sessions and I haven't got time. And I
        can fix the car by myself.
  SEAN: Well, you'll just have to find a way to say no. You can't avoid (14) ....
        to him for ever.

113 *Complete the report by putting the verbs in the correct form, using -ing or to ....*

Cyclist abandons 24 hour ride

ANDREW SPICER, the local cycling star, has decided (1) *to abandon* (abandon) his second attempt (2) .... (ride) non-stop for twenty-four hours. His decision (3) .... (give) up came after poor weather conditions had caused him to delay (4) .... (set) off for several hours. His first attempt had also ended in failure, when he appeared (5) .... (lose) control of his bicycle after he swerved to avoid (6) .... (hit) a small child. He narrowly missed (7) .... (crash) into a gate and ended up in a stream. He says that he has not yet decided whether (8) .... (try) one more time, but denies (9) .... (lose) interest in the project. 'I aim (10) .... (raise) money for the local hospital,' he explains. 'They deserve (11) .... (help) and I shall do it if I can manage (12) .... (find) the time.'

114 *Complete the sentence describing each picture.*

1

Can you help me?

OFFICE

Chris

Terry

Terry wanted ...Chris to help him...

2

Sit!

Angela   Jason

Angela ordered ....

....

3

ROGER HOPKINS

The gangsters forced ....

....

4

I wish I'd never bought those drums.

Laura   Della

Laura regretted ....

....

5

You're not going out until you've finished your homework.

Felicity

Felicity made
....
....
....
....

Charlie

6

SHAMPOO

SOAP

TOOTHPASTE

John

John tried ....

....

7

The car needed ....
....

8

Sandra

Jim

Jim helped ....
....

9

It wasn't us.

Tanya
and Keith

Tanya and Keith denied ....
....

10

Barbara

Barbara dislikes ....
....

11

Betty

*Why don't you
join us?*

Bill and Mandy

Bill and Mandy invited ....
....

115   *Complete the conversations with the correct form of the verbs in brackets and any other essential words.*

A   PAT: Which is the best route into the city centre?

     MICK: It doesn't make much difference, except I'd advise (1) .you not to use.. (not / use) the High
            Street during the rush hour.

B   MARY: Is Mr Wiseman free?

     JOE: Well, there's no one with him, but I wouldn't attempt (2) ....
            (speak) to him now, if I were you. He's in a foul mood.

     MARY: Oh, I don't mind (3) .... (shout) at by him. He threatened
            (4) .... (sack) me last week, but he apologised very politely later.

C   SUE: I don't trust that new cashier.

     JILL: Why not?

     SUE: Well, he claims (5) .... (work) in several other banks before he came
            here, but when I asked him about them he kept (6) .... (change)
            the subject. I was wondering (7) .... (say) something to the manager.

     JILL: Perhaps he's just shy. Why don't we go on (8) .... (be) friendly
            for a few more days and see how he behaves?

     SUE: OK. I must say, I'd hate (9) .... (get) someone into trouble for nothing.

D   ANDY: I don't know what to do about Gemma. She's so difficult to work with. She keeps
            forgetting (10) .... (pass) on important messages, and she won't
            let (11) .... (help) her when she's busy.

     JOAN: Have you actually talked to her about all this?

     ANDY: That's part of the problem. I've tried (12) .... (discuss) the
            problem with her, but she always says she's to busy to stop and talk. I've even tried
            (13) .... (ask) her to have lunch with me, but she doesn't want to.

     JOAN: I think I'd better have a chat with her. How long has she been like this?

     ANDY: Oh, it's several weeks now.

     JOAN: Well, I'd really like (14) .... (know) about the problem earlier.
            Never mind, I'll see what I can do.

     ANDY: Thanks very much.

116   *Complete the sentences with your own ideas, using the **-ing** or **(to) ...** form of a verb.*

1   I never permit .anyone to read.. my diary.

2   I learnt .... at the age of ....

3   I can't help .... when I see someone being treated unfairly.

4   I don't practise .... as regularly as I should.

5   I sometimes pretend .... when really I'm just
    daydreaming.

6   I always encourage .... which I have enjoyed reading myself.

7   I remember .... when I was a small child, but I don't
    remember ...., although my family says I did!

8   I enjoy .... even though I'm not very good at it.

9   I expect .... by the end of next year.

10   I've given up ....

11   I often help ....

Prepositions and expressions + -ing

117

A *Match the two halves of each sentence.*

How to study efficiently
1 Begin by
2 Be realistic: there's no point in
3 Find a quiet place where you can work without
4 If possible, use it only for
5 Check you have everything you need before
6 This means you won't waste time
7 Encourage yourself by

a making plans you can't possibly keep.
b making a list of what you have to do.
c studying.
d marking each topic on your list as you complete it.
e jumping up to fetch things every five minutes.
f being interrupted.
g starting work.

B *Now use the following notes to complete the advice below.*

> *1 Read through the exam paper carefully.*
> *2 Check the instructions.*
> *3 Don't spend too long on one question.*
> *4 Don't try to see how your friends are getting on.*
> *5 Allow time to check all your answers.*
> *6 Cheats rarely do well, in the long run.*

How to take exams
1 Begin .by reading through the exam paper carefully..
2 Make sure you know exactly what to do ....
3 There's no point ....
4 Don't waste ....
5 Avoid careless mistakes ....
6 It's rarely worth ....

118 *Using the **-ing** form, complete the following pieces of advice with your own ideas.*

1 You should take regular exercise instead of .sitting in front of the television all day..
2 You can't earn a lot of money by ....
3 It's rude to borrow people's things without ....
4 You must always thank people for ....
5 You mustn't insist on ....
6 It's wrong to make accusations without ....
7 It's good manners to apologise for ....
8 You should fill up with petrol before ....

I'm used to doing and I used to do

119 *Read the following letter and put the verbs into the correct form.*

Dear Ruth,

Thank you very much for the lovely present you sent for Laurie. It was very kind of you. You say in your note that you haven't got used to (1) ..being.. (be) an aunt yet. I used to (2) ..think.. (think) that becoming a father wouldn't change me. I was wrong, of course! Life will never be the same again. We used to (3) .... (go) to bed at midnight or later. Now we're asleep by ten because we've had to get used to (4) .... (wake) up at five o'clock. Actually, that's quite good in a way. I always used to (5) .... (arrive) late at the office, but since Laurie was born my secretary has got used to (6) .... (find) me hard at work by the time she gets in!

Mind you, it hasn't been so easy for Jenny. I think she found it very hard at first, being with the baby instead of going to work. She wasn't used to (7) .... (spend) all day without adult company. But she's got quite friendly with a neighbour who also has a young baby and I think that makes it easier. She used to (8) .... (say) she'd go back to work when Laurie was six months old, but now she's used to (9) .... (be) at home she's beginning to enjoy herself, so she may wait until Laurie is a bit older.

Anyway, when do you think you'll be able to come and see us? Jenny says hurry up, while Laurie is still small. We'd love a visitor to show her off to!

All the best,

Dennis

Preposition + -ing and to ...

120 *Read and complete the conversations. Use a preposition + -ing (in going / for writing / of doing etc.) or the infinitive (to go / to write / to do etc.).*

A SID: Look, there's Angela. Isn't she lovely?

    TOM: She's all right. You really like her, don't you?

    SID: Oh, yes. I dream (1) ..**of taking**.. (take) her out for a meal or a film, but I'm afraid
(2) ..**to ask**... (her).

    TOM: Why?

    SID: Well, I suppose I'm afraid (3) .... (look) foolish if she refuses.

    TOM: If you like her so much, you shouldn't be afraid (4) .... (risk) it.
Anyway, I'm sure she won't refuse.

    SID: Really? OK. I'll phone her tonight.

    TOM: Good. I'm glad I've succeeded (5) .... (persuade) you to phone
her.

    SID: Why do you say that?

    TOM: I happen to know she rather fancies you. I told her I'd make you phone her! She'll be
looking forward (6) .... (hear) from you!

B BRIAN: Good morning Phil, could we have a word in my office?

    PHIL: Of course.

    BRIAN: I'm sorry (7) .... (have) to tell you, but I'm afraid you failed
(8) .... (achieve) high enough sales to earn a bonus this month. I
suppose it was the bad weather?

    PHIL: Yes, I expect it was. I'm very sorry (9) .... (let) you down.

    BRIAN: OK. I'm sure you'll make it up soon. Actually I'm thinking (10) .... (send)
one or two junior sales staff on a course next month. Would you be interested
(11) .... (go)?

    PHIL: Yes, I would be.

    BRIAN: Good. See you later then

    PHIL: Yes. Thank you. Goodbye.

Verb forms: revision

121 *Can you put the verbs in the correct form **and** solve this detective puzzle?*

TREVOR STERN was not a popular man, in spite of his wealth. He (1) ..**lived**... (live) in a large house about a mile outside the village of Prenton. When he (2) ..**was found**.. (find) dead in his study, no one (3) ...**cried**... (cry), not even his only daughter. It was soon clear that he (4) ....
.... (murder).

Detective Inspector Blackledge took statements from his widow, Dorothy, his seventeen-year-old daughter, Lucy, his business partner, Gerald Brook, and his doctor.

I (5) .... (not/love) my husband, he was a cold and selfish man. But I (6) .... (not/murder) him, either. After dinner last night he said he (7) .... (want) to check some business papers in his study. He (8) .... (have) a meeting with Gerald, his business partner, the next morning. He (9) .... (ask) for some tea. That was about 9 o'clock. I (10) .... (watch) a rather exciting film on television, so I (11) .... (tell) Lucy to take it to him. At quarter past nine Doctor Emerson (12) .... (call). I (13) .... (notice) the time because we (14) .... (expect) him to come earlier. I (15) .... (answer) the front door bell. Trevor (16) .... (still/shout) in his study. He and Lucy (17) .... (obviously/have) a serious row. So I (18) .... (take) the doctor into the sitting-room for a moment. Then Trevor stopped (19) .... (shout). I guessed Lucy (20) .... (go) out by the back door. Doctor Emerson went to the study. I think he wanted to persuade Trevor (21) .... (go) to the hospital for some tests, but Trevor (22) .... (not/want) to go. I (23) .... (hear) him shouting again several times over the next twenty minutes. He called him an ignorant country doctor, and later he said something like 'There's nothing you can do!' I think Lucy (24) .... (come) into the house while the doctor (25) .... (still/talk) to Trevor. I (26) .... (hear) the front door bang during a quiet few seconds when Trevor (27) .... (not/shout). I was tired and fed up and went to my bedroom soon after that. My sister (28) .... (phone) and we (29) .... (talk) for ages. I (30) .... (tell) her I (31) .... (decide) to leave Trevor.

→

Mum (32) .... (watch) some stupid film after dinner, so she made me (33) .... (take) Dad's tea into his study. It was about nine o'clock. He was in a really mean mood. He shouted at me because I (34) .... (spill) a few drops of tea on his desk while I (35) .... (pour) it. I (36) .... (not/want) to watch the film so I (37) .... (creep) out by the back door. I (38) .... (decide) to go down to the village and use the public phone to call Alan. He's my boyfriend. I (39) .... (never/like) Mum or Dad to be around when I (40) .... (talk) to him. Especially yesterday, because Dad and I (41) .... (have) a stupid argument about Alan the day before. It (42) .... (normally/take) quarter of an hour to walk to the village. Perhaps it (43) .... (take) less time last night. I can't prove I (44) .... (go) to the village. No one (45) .... (see) me when I (46) .... (walk) into the village. I (47) .... (see) Gerald, that's Dad's business partner. He (48) .... (stand) near the window in his sitting-room. He (49) .... (not/see) me, though, because it was dark outside. He (50) .... (talk) on the phone, I think.

Alan (51) .... (not/answer) the phone. Then I (52) .... (remember) he (53) .... (tell) me he (54) .... (play) in a concert that evening. So I (55) .... (walk) home again. I (56) .... (meet) Gerald just before I (57) .... (reach) our house. He (58) .... (look) for his dog. That was about twenty to ten. I came in by the back door as quietly as possible and went to bed. I didn't want to see my parents again that evening.

I (59) .... (call) at the Sterns' house at nine-fifteen.
I (60) .... (be) rather later than I (61) ....
.... (plan) to be because I (62) ....
(visit) another patient. When Mrs Stern (63) .... (let)
me into the house she (64) .... (seem)
rather embarrassed and (65) .... (show)
me into the sitting-room. I could hear Trevor Stern
(66) .... (shout) at someone in his study. Mrs
Stern said something about teenage girls and that they (67) ....
.... (have) problems with Lucy. Well, the shouting
(68) .... (stop) almost immediately, so
I (69) .... (go) to his study. Lucy (70) ....
.... (already/leave) the room before I
(71) .... (get) there. I tried
(72) .... (explain) to Trevor why he needed
(73) .... (have) these hospital tests, but he
(74) .... (not/let) me. He said I
(75) .... (be) an ignorant country doctor who
(76) .... (not/know) what he
(77) .... (talk) about. I
(78) .... (realise) it was no use
(79) .... (argue) with him so I
(80) .... (leave) after only a few minutes.
I was quite angry actually. I let myself out of the house without
(81) .... (see) Lucy or Mrs Stern.

Yes, Trevor was my business partner. We (82) ....
.... (not/be) really friends. Yes, my house (83) ....
(be) just round the corner from the Sterns'. I (84) ....
(live) here for two years now. I (85) .... (have)
a little cottage in the village. But I (86) .... (buy)
this house when I started (87) .... (earn) a lot
of money.

I can't really tell you very much about the night Trevor died. I took
my dog for a long walk that evening. I (88) ....
(go) up on the hills, away from the village. Then the stupid dog
(89) .... (go) after a rabbit or something and I
(90) .... (lose) him in the dark. I (91) ....
(look) for him when I (92) .... (meet) Lucy, as
a matter of fact. She (93) .... (walk) up the
road towards their house. She (94) .... (seem)
rather upset. I asked her if she (95) .... (see)
the dog, but she said she (96) .... (not/had).
She (97) .... (go) into her house and
I (98) .... (find) him a few minutes
afterwards. I was back home by just after quarter to ten.

Detective Inspector Blackledge showed the statements to her colleague,
Sergeant Ross.

BLACKLEDGE: Well, Ross. What do you think? Who killed Stern?

ROSS: I don't know. It (99) .... (not/be) his
wife. She (100) .... (not/even/go)
into the study.

BLACKLEDGE: But she admits she didn't love him. Do you think she's in love
with the doctor?

ROSS: It's possible. And perhaps Trevor Stern (101) .... (find out). But we know the doctor was at the hospital by ten o'clock that night. And that's at least half an hour from the Sterns' house.

BLACKLEDGE: But that (102) .... (mean) he (103) .... (leave) the Sterns' house before half past nine.

ROSS: Exactly.

BLACKLEDGE: Anyway, Dorothy Stern told her sister she (104) .... (leave) her husband. She didn't need (105) .... (murder) him.

ROSS: But what about Lucy?

BLACKLEDGE: Yes, there's something about Lucy's story which doesn't quite fit. Let's see, what did Gerald Brook say?

ROSS: That's it! Lucy (106) .... (not/walk) to the village and back, if he (107) .... (meet) her at twenty to ten. She (108) .... (still/shout at) by her father at nine-fifteen.

BLACKLEDGE: But look at all the statements. The times don't fit.

ROSS: Neither do the facts. Someone (109) .... (tell) lies.

BLACKLEDGE: I think it's time we (110) .... (make) an arrest.

Who did they arrest? See page 112.

Countable and uncountable nouns

122   *Write in* **a** *or* **an** *where necessary to make complete sentences, or write* **no change**, *if the sentence is already complete.*

1 Joanna eats apple every morning. ....*an apple*....
2 Peter doesn't like milk in his tea. ..NO CHANGE..
3 Katie rarely has biscuit with her coffee. ....
4 George normally eats meat for dinner. ....
5 Brian usually has omelette for lunch. ....
6 Margaret never drinks beer. ....
7 Robin occasionally puts butter on his potatoes. ....

Jane is trying to lose weight, so everyday she writes down what she has eaten. Look at the picture of what she ate today and complete her notes, using **a** *or* **an** *where necessary.*

Breakfast

Lunch

Dinner

Today was quite good, at least to start with. I only had (8) ..*orange juice*.. *for breakfast. At lunchtime I ate* (9) .... *For dinner I had* (10) .... *and* (11) ...., *followed by* (12) .... *I had* (13) .... *afterwards and I'm afraid I did put* (14) .... *in it!*

123   *Most of these sentences have a mistake in them. Correct them, or if there is no mistake, write* **right**.

1 I believe it's very difficult to find a cheap accommodation in London.
....*to find cheap accommodation*....
2 We're looking for a place to rent. ..RIGHT..
3 We're late because they're re-surfacing the motorway and the traffics are terrible.
....
4 He was asked to leave the college because of a bad behaviour at the end of term party.
....

5 I'm going to phone my brother to wish him good luck for his driving test.

....

6 I think it's a pity Rebecca had her hairs cut short because she looked much more attractive before. ....

7 It's not a bad room, but the furnitures take up too much space. ....

....

8 As an old friend, may I give you an advice? ....

9 If we don't have up-to-date information, how can we make sensible decisions?

....

10 Fortunately, the check-up was less unpleasant experience than I had expected.

....

124 *Fill the spaces in the following conversation with one of the words in the box. Sometimes you need the plural (-s), and some of the words are used more than once.*

~~case~~	day	experience	~~luggage~~	paper
room	scenery	weather	view	

Mary and Liz are about to go on holiday together. Mary has come to collect Liz in her car.

MARY: Hello, Liz, are you ready?

LIZ: Yes, just about. All the (1) ..luggage..... is here in the corridor. I hope I haven't got too many (2) ..cases....

MARY: Don't worry. There's plenty of (3) .... in the car.

LIZ: Oh, good. I've packed rather a lot of things. I haven't had much (4) .... of travelling in the mountains, so I wasn't sure what to bring.

MARY: As long as you've got some warm sweaters for the evenings, and a good raincoat, you should be OK. The (5) .... in the mountains is wonderful, but the (6) .... can change very suddenly.

LIZ: Well, we've got a lovely (7) .... to start with.

MARY: You're right there. And I'm sure you'll like our (8) .... at the hotel, because they've promised me the ones I had last year when I was with my brother. Did you pack the guidebook, by the way?

LIZ: I've got it in my pocket. I packed some (9) .... too, so we can write letters.

MARY: Yes. It'd be nice to keep some sort of diary, too.

LIZ: That's a good idea. We might make an album afterwards, with words and photos. And I'm sure I'm going to have some great (10) .... to write about.

MARY: I'm sure you will, too. The (11) .... are like nothing you've ever seen. And the people are great. There's always music or something in one of the villages every evening. We'll buy some local (12) .... when we get there and find out what's going on this week.

LIZ: Well, I'm ready.

MARY: OK, let's go!

A and an, some and the

125   *Complete the description of this flat with* **a/an**, **some** *or* **the**.

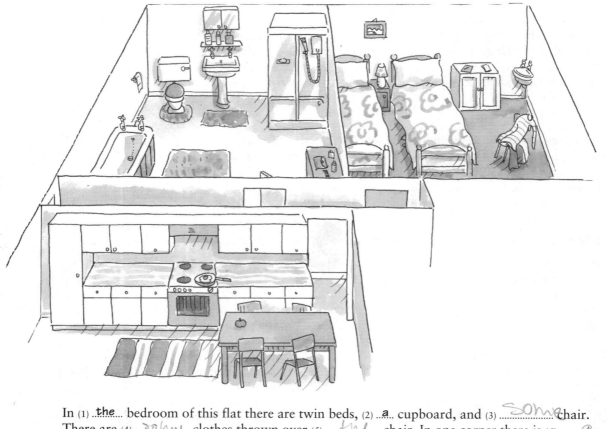

In (1) ..**the**.. bedroom of this flat there are twin beds, (2) ..**a**.. cupboard, and (3) ....*some*.....chair.
There are (4) ....*some*....clothes thrown over (5) .....*the*..... chair. In one corner there is (6) ....*a*......
basin.
    There is also (7) .... basin in (8) .... bathroom. (9) .... basin in (10) ....
bathroom is bigger. Above it there is (11) .... shelf. This flat has (12) .... nice kitchen.
There is (13) .... table with (14) .... chairs round it. In (15) .... middle of
(16) .... table is (17) .... apple.

Now write two more sentences of your own about the flat.

18 ....
19 ....

126 *Put in* **a/an,** *or* **the.**

Tina wants to buy a car. She has come to see Ryan, who is trying to sell his.

TINA: So, you don't say much in your advert. Is this (1) ..**an**.. old car?
RYAN: Four years old. Come and have a look at it.
TINA: Were you (2) .... first owner?
RYAN: No, I got it two years ago.
TINA: Have you driven it a lot?
RYAN: Well, I drive to my office in (3) .... city centre five days (4) .... week, but I don't use it much at weekends.
TINA: I see. Now, the thing is, I'm (5) .... doctor. I've just started work at (6) .... hospital in Hills Road. I'm on call a lot of the time and I have to find (7) .... car which is really reliable. (8) .... car I used to have was always breaking down and giving me problems.
RYAN: Oh, this one's very good. It may not be (9) .... fastest car around, but it always gets there eventually. And it's got (10) .... new set of tyres.
TINA: Right. It's good to know that. Can I go for (11) .... test drive?
RYAN: Um, actually, that's not possible right now.
TINA: Why not?
RYAN: Well, basically, I'm afraid it won't start. You see, (12) .... battery is flat.

The

127 *Put in* **the** *where necessary. If* **the** *is not needed, leave a space* (–).

Portrait of a family: (1) ..The.. Bartons

There are three adults and two children in this family. (2) ..The.. children are Ben, aged twelve, and (3) ..–.. little Stella, who is four. Their parents are Andrew and Marion. (4) .... other adult is Leslie, who is Andrew's brother. He is twenty-four. They live in Newcastle, a large city in (5) .... north-east of England.

On (6) .... weekday mornings everyone gets up early. Andrew Barton works for a company which manufactures (7) .... computers. He leaves at seven o'clock. He likes to avoid (8) .... rush hour, he says. Marion suspects that really he likes to avoid having breakfast with (9) .... children, who are very noisy.

Ben catches (10) .... school bus at eight-fifteen. Leslie is at (11) .... university, studying physics. He lives away from (12) .... home during term-time, so he avoids (13) .... noise, too.

Stella doesn't go to (14) .... school yet, of course. Next year, she will start at (15) .... nursery school where Ben used to go. Her mother is looking forward to this, as it will mean that she can go back to (16) .... work. Before her marriage, she lived in London, where she worked for (17) .... National Gallery, in (18) .... Trafalgar Square. She is hoping to find (19) .... same sort of job in Newcastle.

128 *In the following news items* **the** *has sometimes been used in the wrong place. Read them carefully and cross out* **the** *where it is not necessary.*

The Prime Minister left this morning for a tour of the Far East. He will visit ~~the~~ Singapore and the Malaysia and then go on to the Philippines, where he will make a speech about the environment.

The King Juan Carlos of ~~the~~ Spain arrived in London today for a three day visit to the United Kingdom. He was met by the Queen and drove with her to the Buckingham Palace. Tomorrow he will have ~~the~~ lunch with the Governor of the Bank of England and in ~~the~~ evening he will have talks with ~~the~~ businessmen.

A CONFERENCE is taking place in the Mexico City on ways of helping the unemployed in the developing world. A report will be sent to the United Nations, but it is feared that the unemployment will remain a problem in the most countries for many years to come.

Quantifiers and pronouns

129

While you were shopping, some thieves stole your wallet. You saw them, but they got away. Complete the description you gave to the police.

1 All ..*of them have fair hair.*..
2 None ..*of them was older than thirty.*...
3 Both ..*the men were wearing t-shirts.*...
4 One ..*of the men had a shoulder bag.*.....
5 All ....
6 None ....
7 Both ....
8 Both ....
9 Both ....
10 Neither ....
11 Neither ....
12 One ....

130 *Use the words in the first box to make true statements about the people in the second box.*

all (of)	most of	lots of	some of	(a) few of
none of	both (of)	neither of	one of	

grandfathers	neighbours	doctors	cousins
classmates	bands	politicians	students
relatives	parents	friends	

1 Most of the students in my class like rock music.
2 Both of my grandfathers were farmers.
3 One of the bands I admire is U2.
4 Few of my friends wear high heels.
5 ....
6 ....
7 ....
8 ....
9 ....

131 *Choose the correct words from the box to complete the sentences.*

few (of)	a few (of)	none (of)	any (of)	half (of)
all (of)	each (of)	much (of)	most (of)	

1 It is widely believed that ..all.. human beings are descended from one common ancestor.
2 When Jill decided to sell her car she phoned round her friends, but .... them wanted to buy it so she put an ad in the paper.
3 .... people enjoy housework.
4 When my rich uncle died, he left .... his fortune to his cat and the other half to a distant cousin! We had never expected to receive .... it, but we were disappointed that he hadn't left .... it to us.
5 I think .... children enjoy going to funfairs, although I know .... who are frightened of the big rides.
6 We'll have to work quickly because I haven't got .... time.
7 Before mixing the cake, weigh .... ingredient precisely.

132 *Choose the correct word or phrase to fill each space in this passage.*

Last week I made the mistake of revisiting the village where I grew up. It was a small, friendly community with two farms and a number of old cottages round the village green. I realised very quickly that although in (1) <u>many / ~~few~~</u> ways it appears unchanged, in reality hardly (2) <u>nothing / anything</u> is the same. (3) <u>All / Every</u> the pretty cottages are there, of course, and (4) <u>both / most</u> the picturesque farmhouses. But (5) <u>none of the / none of</u> inhabitants are country people. All of (6) <u>they / them</u> are commuters, who leave early (7) <u>every morning / all the mornings</u> for the nearby town. (8) <u>Neither of / Neither</u> the farmhouses is attached to a farm these days; the land has been sold and is managed by (9) <u>somebody / anyone</u> in an office (10) <u>anywhere / somewhere</u> who has (11) <u>little / a little</u> interest in the village itself. There are (12) <u>few / a few</u> new houses, but they have (13) <u>no / none of</u> local character; you can see the same style (14) <u>anywhere / somewhere</u> in the country. (15) <u>The whole / Whole</u> of the village, in fact, has been tidied up so much that it has become (16) <u>anything / nothing</u> more than just another suburb.

133 *Find the mistakes and correct them. If there is no mistake, write* **right**.

1 He shouted at all of students although most of us had done nothing wrong.
   .**He shouted at all of the students....**.
2 Can anyone use the tennis courts or only college students? .**RIGHT**.
3 What happens if anybody get left behind when the coach leaves?
   ....
4 What a boring town! There are not good restaurants, nothing!
   ....
5 I think he was lonely because he had a few friends and none of his neighbours ever spoke to him. ....
6 We can't use this room because there are no chairs in it. ....
7 I've wasted two hours because the whole information you gave me was wrong.
   ....
8 When I got on the plane the steward told me I could have some seat because there were so few passengers on the flight. ....
9 You can't borrow money from me because I have no. My brother's already borrowed it all.
   ....
10 The problem is that I have much homework to do at weekends, so I have very little time for sport. ....
11 I don't know whether our scheme will in fact make a profit, but any money we do raise will be given to charity. ....
12 I feel so embarrassed that all know my problem. I wish you hadn't said anything.
   ....

Relative clauses

134 *Can you answer the questions about the people in Box A, using information from Boxes B and C?*

A

1 Who was Alexander Fleming?
2 Who was Antonio Stradivari?
3 Who was Ibn Battuta?
4 Who was Johann Gutenberg?
5 Who was Joseph Lister?
6 Who was Orville Wright?
7 Who was Joseph Niepce?

Alexander Fleming

Antonio Stradivari

Joseph Lister

Johann Gutenberg

Joseph Niepce

Ibn Battuta

B

American	Englishman	
Frenchman	German	
Italian	Moroccan	Scotsman

C

He travelled through Africa and Asia.
He made wonderful violins.
He discovered penicillin.
He constructed the first mechanical printing press.
He began the use of antiseptics in operating theatres.
He produced the first permanent photograph.
He flew the first real aeroplane.

Orville Wright

1 Alexander Fleming was a Scotsman who discovered penicillin.
2 ....
3 ....
4 ....
5 ....
6 ....
7 ....

135 *Complete the conversation with* **who**, **that**, **whose**, *or* **where**. *If no word is needed, leave a space* (—).

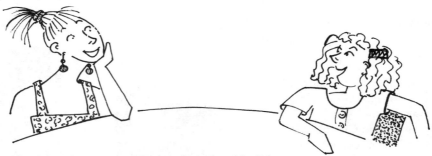

Zoe and Pat are planning a party during the school holidays.

ZOE: Well, who shall we ask to this party?

PAT: Oh, not too many. Just a few people (1) ..—... we can be relaxed with.

ZOE: Yes, I agree. So, who, for example?

PAT: My cousin John, of course, and Carlo.

ZOE: Carlo? Who's he?

PAT: He's the Italian guy (2) ..who.... is staying with John's family.

ZOE: Oh, yeah. Is he the one (3) .... wallet got stolen when they were in London?

PAT: That's right. They caught the guy (4) .... did it, but he'd already spent all the money (5) .... Carlo had brought with him.

ZOE: Poor Carlo. Perhaps the party will cheer him up.

PAT: It might, if we ask the girl (6) .... he's been going out with.

ZOE: Who's that?

PAT: Celia's her name. She works in that cinema (7) .... they show all the foreign films.

ZOE: But will she be free on Thursday evening?

PAT: Yes, it's her evening off. That's the reason (8) .... I suggested Thursday.

ZOE: OK. Who else? What about Nicky and Cherry?

PAT: Are they the girls (9) .... you went to France with?

ZOE: Yes. If they bring their boyfriends, that'll be ten of us. But have you got a room (10) .... is big enough? My mother says we can't use our sitting-room because we made too much mess the last time (11) .... she let us have a party.

PAT: It's all right. We've got a basement (12) .... we store old furniture. If we clean it up, it'll be fine.

ZOE: Great. Let's go and have a look at it.

136 *Match each situation with one of the sentences that follow.*

A   1 I have three umbrellas. I bought one of them in Paris. That one needs repairing. ..a....
        a The umbrella which I bought in Paris needs repairing.
        b The umbrella, which I bought in Paris, needs repairing.

    2 I have one colleague. He works extremely hard. He has few friends. ..b....
        a My colleague who works extremely hard is not very popular.
        b My colleague, who works extremely hard, is not very popular.

    3 I have several aunts. One works in New York. She's getting married. ....
        a My aunt who works in New York is getting married.
        b My aunt, who works in New York, is getting married.

4 Peter made some sandwiches. They have all been eaten. You made some too. Your
   sandwiches have not been eaten. ....
  a The sandwiches which Peter made have all been eaten.
  b The sandwiches, which Peter made, have all been eaten.

5 There was only one park in this town. Someone has built over it. We used to play in the
   park when we were children. ....
  a The local park where we played as children has been built over.
  b The local park, where we played as children, has been built over.

6 One of my French teachers helps me with my homework. The other one lives too far
   away. ....
  a The French teacher whose house is near mine helps me with my homework.
  b The French teacher, whose house is near mine, helps me with my homework.

7 You met one of my cousins last summer, the one from America. He's coming to stay
   again. ....
  a My American cousin who you met last summer is coming to stay again.
  b My American cousin, who you met last summer, is coming to stay again.

8 There were a lot of candidates in the presidential election. Three of them were women. The
   winner was one of them. She had campaigned for better housing conditions. ....
  a The woman who led the campaign for better housing conditions has been elected
    President.
  b The woman, who led the campaign for better housing conditions, has been elected
    President.

9 Only my boyfriend sent me flowers, but I had some other presents, including a vase. I put
   the flowers in the vase. ....
  a The flowers which my boyfriend sent look beautiful in my new vase.
  b The flowers, which my boyfriend sent, look beautiful in my new vase.

10 I took two cameras away with me. You lent me one of them. That's the one that got
   broken. ....
  a The camera which you lent me has been broken.
  b The camera, which you lent me, has been broken.

B *Now describe the situations for some of the other sentences in 136A.*

1 I have an umbrella. It needs repairing. I bought it in Paris.
2 I work with several colleagues. There's one who works extremely hard, but no one likes him much.
3 ....
4 ....
5 ....
6 ....

137 *Complete the sentences with a word or phrase from the box and your own ideas.*

which	~~which~~	which	~~who~~
who	to whom	whose	where

1 I like meeting people ..who have travelled widely....
2 I enjoy parties ..which go on till dawn...
3 I avoid going to restaurants ...*which are too expensive*
4 Most of my friends are people ...*who have children*
5 I never wear clothes ...*which make me feel uncomfortable*
6 My favourite films are those ...*which have plenty action*
7 I feel sorry for children ...*who parents argue*
8 My best friend is someone ...*to whom i can say anything*

Adjectives and adverbs

138 *Rewrite each sentence beginning with the words given.*

1 Ursula is a very quick learner.
  Ursula learns ..very quickly...
2 Richard can cook really well.
  Richard is a ....
3 Your behaviour was extremely foolish.
  You behaved ....
4 The hotel staff treated us in a very friendly manner.
  The hotel staff were ....
5 I don't think that's a practical suggestion.
  That suggestion doesn't sound ....
6 Philippa is usually a hard worker.
  Philippa usually works ....
7 Have the children been good today?
  Have the children behaved ....?
8 I wish you could swim fast.
  I wish you were ....

The language school is very efficiently organised. On the first morning we had to do a test, which I found rather haddly. However, I got a surprisingly good mark so I'm in second class.

Aren't you impressed at how accurate my English is now?

139 *Choose the correct form from each pair of words.*

> Dear Natasha,
>   Well, here I am in England. Thank you for your (1) *kind/~~kindly~~* letter.
> You ask me what it's like here. I must say, it's pretty (2) *good/~~well~~*! The
> language school is very (3) *~~efficient~~/efficiently* organised. On the first morning
> we had to do a test, which I found rather (4) *hard/~~hardly~~*. However I got a
> (5) *~~surprising~~/surprisingly* good mark, so I'm in the second class. I didn't talk
> much at first, because I couldn't think of the words (6) *~~quick~~/quickly* enough,
> but (7) *~~late~~/lately* I've become much more (8) *~~fluent~~/fluently*. I'm staying with a
> family who live (9) *near/~~nearly~~* the school. They are quite
> (10) *pleasant/~~pleasantly~~*, although I don't see much of them because I'm always
> so (11) *busy/~~busily~~* with my friends from school. I was surprised how
> (12) *~~easy~~/easily* I made new friends here. They come from
> (13) *different/~~differently~~* parts of the world and we have some
> (14) *~~absolute~~/absolutely* fascinating discussions. I do hope you will be able to
> join me here next term. I'm sure we'd have (15) *good/~~well~~* fun together.
>   All the best,
>   Misha
> P.S. Aren't you impressed at how (16) *~~accurate~~/accurately* my English is now?!

140 *Find the mistakes and correct them. If there is no mistake, write* **right***.*

1 'Please get a move on!' shouted Trevor impatient. ....'Please get a move on!' shouted Trevor
  ..impatiently...

2 I believe she is a very lonely woman. ..RIGHT..

3 I didn't like his plan, which seemed unnecessary complicated to me.
  ....

4 I'm sure you could win the match if you tried hardly.
  ....

5 I have an awful headache, so could you please be quiet.
  ....

6 Soraya's only been in France a year, but she speaks perfectly French.
  ....

7 The reason Bruce gets so tired is that he has an exceptional demanding job.
  ....

8 My mother was very ill last year, but she's good enough to go on holiday now.
  ....

9 David ran as fast as he could but he still arrived late. ....

10 In spite of the fact that Jean always says she's short of money, I happen to know she actually
   has a very good-paid job. ....

Comparatives and superlatives

141 *A class of students is studying environmental issues with their teacher. Look at the diagram and complete their conversation.*

TEACHER: Who recycled (1) ..the highest.. percentage of glass in 1992?

FLORA: The Dutch did.

TEACHER: And who recycled (2) .... percentage?

WAYNE: The Greeks.

TEACHER: Right. What about the Spanish? How well did they do?

JILL: They did (3) .... the Greeks, but (4) .... the Portuguese.

TEACHER: Did the French recycle a (5) .... percentage of glass .... the Danes?

KEVIN: No, not quite. About five per cent (6) ....

TEACHER: What about the Italians?

BRONWEN: They recycled about (7) .... percentage .... the Belgians.

TEACHER: Yes. That's about five per cent (8) .... the Danes.

ALEX: But it's about ten per cent (9) .... the Germans.

TEACHER: True. Now let's go on to talk about what we're going to do next.

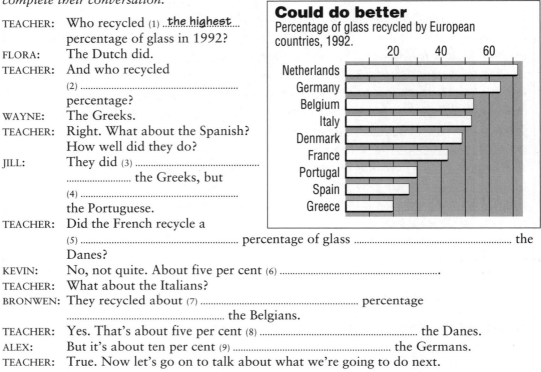

Could do better
Percentage of glass recycled by European countries, 1992.

20 40 60

Netherlands
Germany
Belgium
Italy
Denmark
France
Portugal
Spain
Greece

The class took part in a paper recycling project. Look at the table below and write sentences comparing the students' achievements.

Flora 50 Kilos · Kevin 45 Kilos · Jill 30 Kilos · Bronwen 30 Kilos · Alex 25 Kilos · Wayne 10 Kilos

10 Kevin / Flora / Jill .Kevin didn't collect as much paper as Flora, but he collected more than Jill.

11 Alex / Bronwen / Jill .Alex collected five kilos less than Bronwen or Jill.

12 Flora .Flora collected the most paper.

13 Jill / Alex / Wayne ....

14 Bronwen / Jill ....

15 Wayne ....

16 Alex / Bronwen / Wayne ....

17 Jill / Flora / Alex ....

142   *Complete the conversations, using the correct form of the word(s) supplied and adding any other words needed.*

A   JOE: Why have you bought a new car?

     AMY: We needed one with a (1) .**bigger**.... (big) boot, to take our sports gear.

B   ANDY: Are you still trying to get that stain out of the rug?

     JENNY: Yes. I don't know what it is. I've tried all sorts of soaps and things but it's still
(2) .**no cleaner than**.... (clean) when I started.

C   ROSE: Do you happen to know which is (3) ..**the smallest planet**.. (small / planet) in our solar system?

     JILL: Pluto, isn't it? I know it's (4) .**the furthest**.... (far) away from the sun.

D   FRED: How was your driving test?

     GEORGE: Oh, not so bad really. It was (5) .... (much / easy) I'd expected, in fact.

     FRED: So, you've passed?

     GEORGE: Yes, I have.

     FRED: Congratulations! That's (6) .... (good) news I've heard for ages!

E   MARY: Which is (7) .... (high / mountain) in Africa?

     ANNE: I'm not sure. Kilimanjaro, perhaps?

     MARY: Where's that? In Zambia?

     ANNE: No, it's (8) .... (far / north) that. Kenya I think.

F   GAIL: Shall we go for a swim? It's lovely and sunny.

     MICK: I'm not sure. There's quite a strong wind. I think you'll find it's (9) ....
.... (not / warm) it looks, when you get outside.

G   EDDY: We'd better go to the bank this morning.

     SEAN: Can't we go (10) .... (late) ?

     EDDY: No. They shut (11) .... (early / here) they do at home.

H   WILL: Hurry up! We'll miss the train. Can't you run
(12) .... (fast) ?

     PETE: Sorry, I'm going (13) .... (fast) I can already.

     WILL: OK. I guess you're quite a bit (14) .... (short / I) after all.

I   CHRIS: I hear you were having problems with your business last year. Is it
(15) .... (good) this year?

     CLARE: No. I'm afraid it's (16) .... (bad) if anything.

     CHRIS: I suppose people just aren't spending (17) ....
(much / money) they used to.

Word order – adverbs with the verb

143 *Make sentences about the three people in the left-hand column, using the words in each row with the adverbs at the top.*

	occasionally	*usually*	*hardly ever*
Angela	arrives at work early	isn't in the office at lunch-time	has taken a day off
John	is late for work	won't do overtime	has sandwiches for lunch
Craig	has offered to work through lunch	leaves later than everyone else	is ill

1 Angela occasionally arrives at work early.
2 John is occasionally late for work.
3 ....
4 ....
5 ....
6 ....
7 ....
8 ....
9 ....

144 *Rewrite the sentences in **bold type** including the adverbs in brackets at the end.*

Andy and Jane came home from shopping on Saturday to find their house had been burgled. Mary is a police officer who has come to investigate the crime.

MARY: Now, you say you're not sure how the thieves got in. Before I look round, can I ask you a few questions about the house?

ANDY: Of course.

MARY: **Do you lock the front door when you go out?** (always)
(1) Do you always lock the front door?

ANDY: Yes, and **I locked it yesterday.** (definitely) (2) I definitely locked it yesterday.

MARY: OK. What about the windows?

ANDY: Well, **the downstairs ones are locked.** (always)
(3) ....

JANE: **We have a lock on the little one in the hall.** (even)
(4) ....

MARY: And upstairs?

JANE: Well, I think **most of the windows were locked.** (probably)
(5) ....

ANDY: **They were locked on Friday.** (all) (6) ....

JANE: Are you sure?

ANDY: Yes. I checked them all because **I knew we would be out all day.** (both)
(7) ....
MARY: And you didn't open any on Friday night?
ANDY: No. **I didn't.** (definitely) (8) ....
MARY: Well, I can't understand it. Let's go and look round. Perhaps I'll notice something you've missed.

145 *Answer the questions with the words given.*

1 What does Timothy have for breakfast?
   (has an egg + usually) .He. usually. has. an. egg....
2 Does Margaret watch a lot of television.
   (doesn't own one + even) .She. doesn't. even. own. one.....
3 Why did James leave the party.
   (was bored + probably) He ....
4 Does Sally like your house?
   (has been there + never) She ....
5 Do you know where Maureen might be?
   (has a rest about this time + often) She ....
6 How is Keith getting on with his homework?
   (has finished it + almost) He ....
7 Is Donald coming to the wedding?
   (hasn't been invited + even) He ....
8 Why do Robert and George hate each other?
   (want to marry Alice + both) They ....

Prepositions of time

146 *Complete the sentences with* **during, by, until, at, on** *or* **in.** *If no word is needed, leave a space (–).*

1 We usually finish work early ..on... Fridays.
2 .... the time you get this letter, I shall be in Miami.
3 She wrote this article .... her holiday.
4 He won't hand over the parcel .... we pay him.
5 The children aren't here .... the moment, but they'll be back ....
   a few minutes.
6 Can you come to tea with us .... next Sunday?
7 I want to be at the stadium early so that we're .... time to get good seats.
8 Please don't touch anything .... the police arrive.
9 I should be free by 3 p.m. If the meeting doesn't end .... time, I shall have to
   make my apologies and leave.
10 She was reluctant to help us at first, but .... the end she agreed to do what she
   could.
11 I'm not sure whether it'll be Thursday or Friday, but I'll definitely be back ....
   the weekend.
12 Will you finish work .... time to do the shopping?
13 We always used to have a party .... the end of term.
14 I'd like to hold our next meeting .... 23rd March. Will that suit you?

147 *Complete the description with* at, for, during, by, until *or* in.

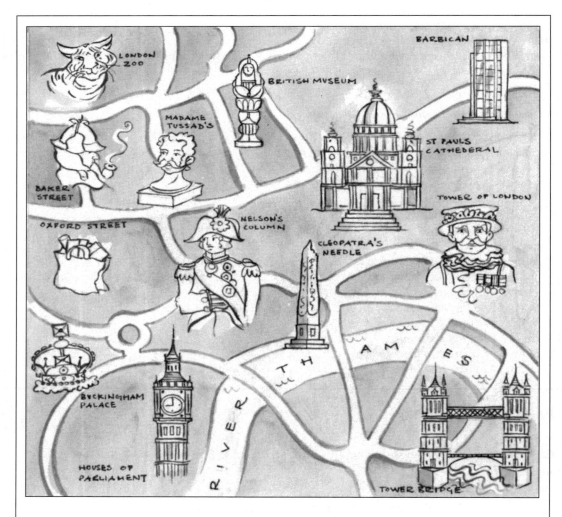

The city of London was founded by the Romans (1) ..in...the year 43 AD.
(2) .During.. the next few years it quickly became the main trading centre in Britain. (3) .... two hundred years after the Romans left, the city was almost forgotten. Its full importance did not return (4) .... the eleventh century. (5) .... the end of that century, the government of England was based in Westminster and the Tower of London had been started. (6) .... the Middle Ages London continued to grow, and (7) .... the time of Shakespeare it had become a prosperous capital city with many fine buildings. Unfortunately, most of these buildings were made of wood and (8) .... 1666 they were almost all destroyed by a fire which lasted (9) .... several days. This was a great tragedy for the people living there (10) .... that time, but it is true that many of the areas which are most attractive today were planned (11) .... the rebuilding which followed.

148 *Complete the following description with* for, during, by, until, at, in *or* on.

Eleanor is a nurse who works the night shift.
How does she manage?

'Well I finish work (1) ..at.. 6.30 a.m. Then I go home, have a bath and try to be in bed (2) ..by.. half past eight.
(3) .... the same time as I'm getting ready for bed, Jeffrey, my husband, and our five-year-old daughter, Elaine, are getting up. Jeffrey takes her to nursery school. I usually sleep (4) .... about 3 o'clock (5) .... the afternoon. I have to be at the school (6) .... 3.30, to collect Elaine. We come home and I play with her, and try to get some housework done (7) .... the same time. When my husband comes home, we eat. If I'm lucky, I can relax (8) .... an hour before putting Elaine to bed.

Then I do some of the housework that didn't get done (9) .... the day. I allow plenty of time to get to the hospital because if I'm not there (10) .... time, another nurse will have to go on working (11) .... I arrive. I'm often very tired (12) .... the time I finish, but I don't really mind. There's a special atmosphere in the hospital (13) .... night. And the hours suit us, (14) .... the moment, anyway.

I may want to work days when Elaine goes to a different school. Perhaps I'll be ready for a change (15) .... then.'

Prepositions of place

149 *Choose the correct words in the conversations.*

A JAY: Oh, look. Here's a photo taken in my classroom at primary school. Can you recognise
me (1) <u>in</u> / <s>on</s> it?
ANNA: No, I don't think so. Unless that's you right (2) <u>in</u> / <u>at</u> the back.
JAY: No, that's not me. I'm the one standing (3) <u>in</u> / <u>at</u> the corner.
ANNA: In trouble as usual!

B PIA: I don't understand this.
LILY: What?
PIA: Well, I want to check something with the college, but it says (4) <u>in</u> / <u>on</u> this letter that I
must give a reference number when I phone, and I can't find it.
LILY: It's in that little booklet, (5) <u>in</u> / <u>on</u> the first page.
PIA: Oops! So it is. Thanks.

C LEN: Where's your sister?
SUE: She's (6) <u>at</u> / <u>in</u> a wedding.
LEN: Oh? Where?
SUE: (7) <u>At</u> / <u>In</u> Paris.
LEN: Who's getting married?
SUE: She is.
LEN: Oh.

D GARY: What was that?
NICK: What?
GARY: I'm sure I saw a face (8) <u>at</u> / <u>in</u> the window.
NICK: Don't be silly. It's the television, reflected (9) <u>on</u> / <u>in</u> the glass.

E MEL: Did you see Yves (10) <u>in</u> / <u>at</u> the dance?
JAN: No, of course not. He went back (11) <u>to</u> / <u>in</u> France last week.
MEL: But I'm sure I saw him (12) <u>in</u> / <u>on</u> the bus yesterday. In fact, he waved to me when we
arrived (13) <u>to</u> / <u>at</u> the bus station.
JAN: How strange. We'll have to investigate what he's up to!

150   *Complete the note with* **in**, **on** *or* **at**.

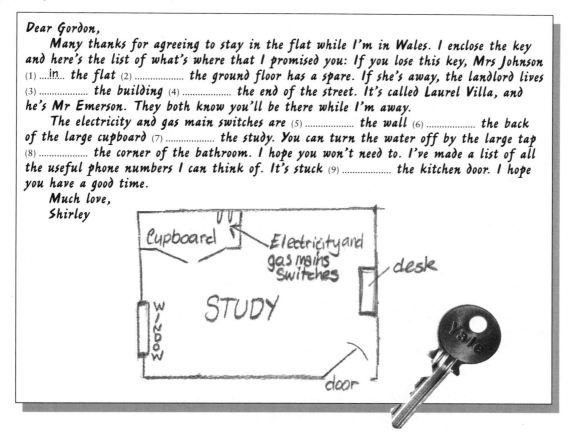

Dear Gordon,
    Many thanks for agreeing to stay in the flat while I'm in Wales. I enclose the key
and here's the list of what's where that I promised you: If you lose this key, Mrs Johnson
(1) ...**in**.. the flat (2) .... the ground floor has a spare. If she's away, the landlord lives
(3) .... the building (4) .... the end of the street. It's called Laurel Villa, and
he's Mr Emerson. They both know you'll be there while I'm away.
    The electricity and gas main switches are (5) .... the wall (6) .... the back
of the large cupboard (7) .... the study. You can turn the water off by the large tap
(8) .... the corner of the bathroom. I hope you won't need to. I've made a list of all
the useful phone numbers I can think of. It's stuck (9) .... the kitchen door. I hope
you have a good time.
    Much love,
    Shirley

Prepositions (general)

Units 116 and 126–128

151   *Choose the correct prepositions.*

Trouble at Norton Mining

The entire workforce of Norton Mining has gone (1) <u>on</u>/~~in~~ strike following a serious accident at the mine in Coolooma. The cause (2) <u>for/of</u> the accident is unclear, but the union is blaming management attitudes (3) <u>on/to</u> safety regulations. A spokesperson said 'Damage (4) <u>of/to</u> equipment was frequently ignored and union demands (5) <u>for/of</u> safer working practices were rejected. The managers' relationship (6) <u>with/to</u> the union was very poor, so although we pointed out that there'd been a rise (7) <u>of/in</u> the number of minor accidents over the past year, they said there was no need (8) <u>for/of</u> a change in working practices.'

John Norton, the chairman of Norton Mining, is away (9) <u>on/in</u> a business trip. His secretary said she had spoken to him (10) <u>by/on</u> the phone. The news of the accident had come (11) <u>like/as</u> a great shock to him, she added. She was unable to say when he would be back.

It is understood that the police would like to speak to Mr Norton in connection (12) <u>with/to</u> a number of his financial dealings.

152 *Complete the answers to the questions. Use one of the prepositions in the box with the words provided and any other necessary words.*

as	at	by	in	like	on

1 What's this room?
   (store room) We use it ..*as a store room.*..
2 Where's Geraldine?
   (holiday) She's ..*on holiday.*...
3 What would you like to do now?
   (shade) Let's sit ....
4 Why aren't you eating any cake?
   (diet) I'm ....
5 Can you really afford to buy that CD player now?
   (credit card) It's OK. I'll pay ....
6 Surely they didn't drive all the way to Istanbul?
   (plane) No, they travelled ....
7 Was the exhibition interesting?
   (little-known Russian artists) Yes. The works were all ....
8 Why were so many people injured in the crash?
   (130 kilometres an hour) Because the train was travelling ....
9 Why are you writing so slowly?
   (capital letters) Because I have to put my address ....
10 Can you ring to let me know you're home safely?
   (phone) Not very easily. You see, I'm not ....
11 What was the course like?
   (whole) Some parts were a bit dull, but it wasn't bad ....
12 How do you get on with your father?
   (best friend) I regard him ....
13 Why is your hand so swollen?
   (wasp) I got stung ....
14 What sort of car has Christine bought this time?
   (the last one) A Ford, ...
15 Where's the fax machine?
   (photocopier) In the office, ...
16 What are you doing in the summer holidays?
   (motorcycle messenger) I've got a job ....
17 Why were you so late?
   (fog) We got lost ....
18 Why does Andrew keep making mistakes?
   (love) He must be ....

Adjective/verb + preposition

Units 129–135

153 *Find the mistakes and correct them. If there is no mistake write* **right.**

1 It wasn't very sensible in you to leave your anorak at home in this weather.
...... very sensible of you ......

2 She's only crying because she wants you to feel sorry for her. Ignore her and she'll stop.
.. RIGHT ..

3 When he had explained me what he was looking for, I was able to help him.
.... explained to me .....

4 Be quiet. I don't want to discuss about the matter any more. .... discuss the matter .....

5 Joanna was very proud to her son when he won the race. ....

6 I don't think I'll come with you. I'm not really interested of folk music.

....

7 That man's smiling at me as if he knows me. ....

8 One of the boys threw a bottle to the car and broke the windscreen.

....

9 Mrs Mackenzie claimed she'd been sent by the local council, but when I phoned to check they said they'd never heard about such a person. ....

10 I'll make sure he gets the message before he leaves to the office in the morning.

....

11 How dare you accuse me of stealing? I wouldn't dream of doing such a thing!

....

12 It's no good complaining about the problem if you're not prepared to do anything for it.

....

13 He's one of those people who believes by saying what he thinks, even when it upsets people.

....

14 After receiving a tip-off, the customs officers searched to the car for drugs.

....

15 I'm so bored of this exercise I could scream. ....

16 Are you nervous about addressing a large audience? ....

17 I'm afraid your teacher was rather shocked for what I said. ....

18 I was furious at first, but after he had apologised me I calmed down.

....

154 *Match the two halves of these sentences.*

A 1 He hasn't forgiven her   a on her to help me.
  2 I no longer care   b for what she did.
  3 I'm old enough to look   c of managing alone.
  4 She's perfectly capable   d in changing her opinion.
  5 He'll never succeed   e after myself.
  6 I'm relying   f about what he thinks.

B 1 The lorry collided   a of market stalls.
  2 The bus crashed   b with a line of cars.
  3 The square was full   c from a local family.
  4 The minibus belonged   d on a pedestrian.
  5 They borrowed the car   e into the railings.
  6 They blamed the accident   f to a group of tourists.

Phrasal verbs

155   *Complete the answers to these questions.*

1   NINA: What shall I do with this form?
      JOHN: Just fill .it in. and send it to the address at the top.
2   FRED: Is Sonia a fast runner?
      SUE: Oh, yes. Nobody else can keep ....
3   ALAN: Why didn't you buy a dictionary?
      DAVE: The bookshop has run ....
4   MAY: Did you believe Nicola's story?
      EVAN: No, I knew she must have made ....
5   GREG: Do we need to finish this drawing before the meeting?
      BILL: Yes, we do, so you'd better get ....
6   CILLA: What are the girls doing in the garden with the tent?
      ALEC: They want to put .... before they go away, to check that it's OK.
7   LEE: Were you disappointed that Graham missed the meeting?
      RUTH: Yes, we all felt he'd let .... rather badly.
8   IAN: Did Francesca play with her cousins when they came to stay?
      JIM: Oh, yes. She got .... very well.

156   *Rewrite the sentences replacing the <u>underlined</u> verbs with the correct form of one of the verbs in the box. Use your dictionary if necessary.*

carry on	find out	go in for	~~look back on~~	own up
put up with	~~set off~~	stand up for	think over	turn down

1   I'm sure we'll all <u>remember</u> this holiday with great pleasure.
   ... **we'll all look back on this holiday** ...
2   The fireworks must be stored safely in order to avoid <u>exploding</u> them accidentally.
   ... **in order to avoid setting them off accidentally.** ...
3   I didn't expect to win the competition. I only <u>entered</u> it for a joke.
....
4   Unless you <u>confess</u>, we shall all be punished.
....
5   Before you accept this offer, please <u>consider</u> it very carefully.
....
6   We can't <u>continue</u> if you won't co-operate.
....
7   When the critics attacked her work she <u>defended</u> it vigorously.
....
8   He was offered a new job but he <u>refused</u> it because he didn't want to move house.
....
9   We moved house because we couldn't <u>bear</u> the noise from the motorway any longer.
....
10   He had to leave when his boss <u>discovered</u> what he had been doing.
....

Spelling

157 *Put the nouns into groups to show how they form plurals.*

book	match	baby	brick	play	spy
kiss	party	tax	berry	moth	bus
query	brush	ghost	guy	pony	march

1 + s
book/books
....
....
....
....
....

2 + es
match/matches
....
....
....
....
....

3 y + ies
baby/babies
....
....
....
....
....

158 *Put the verbs into groups to show how the **-ing** form is spelt. The groups will not be the same size.*

employ	argue	forget	chatter	fail	worry
free	rebel	plant	reply	stare	refer
love	despair	refuse	stay	admit	swim
widen	invade	rub	consider		

1 + ing
employ/employing
....
....
....
....
....
....
....
....
....
....

2 e + ing
argue/arguing
....
....
....
....
....
....
....
....
....
....

3 double letter + ing
forget/forgetting
....
....
....
....
....
....
....
....
....
....

ACKNOWLEDGEMENTS

The authors and the publishers are grateful to the following individuals and institutions for permission to reproduce copyright material.

Photographs
The Ronald Grant Archive: p.9; Pictor International for the pyramid and the Statue of Liberty: p.56; Giraudon, The Prado, Madrid and the Bridgeman Art Library for *Guernica* by Pablo Picasso, © DACS 1995: p.56; Penguin Books Limited for the cover illustration of *Animal Farm* by George Orwell, © Christopher Corr 1994: p.56; The Blakeney Hotel, Norfolk p.65; Allsport p.76; Sally and Richard Greenhill Photo Library: p81; Nigel Luckhurst pp. 91 and 107; Photobank: p.94; Barnaby's Picture Library for Sir Joseph Lister, Johann Gutenberg and Dr Alex Fleming: p.95; Mary Evans Picture Library for Antonio Stradivari: p.95; Popperfoto for Orville Wright: p.95; The Mansell Collection for Joseph Niepce: p.95; Format Partners Photo Library: p.105.

Drawings
Amanda McPhail: pp. 6, 7, 8, 9, 13, 15, 16, 22, 31, 32, 37, 43, 48, 49, 51, 53, 54, 56, 57, 58, 64, 68, 69, 70, 72, 73, 77, 78, 92, 96, 100; Bill Piggins: pp. 11, 19, 23, 41, 50, 66, 71 (top), 82, 83, 84, 85, 86, 87, 90; David Downton: p.28; Abbas Hashemi for the double helix: p.56; Leslie Marshall for the wireless: p.56; Peter Ducker for the map of Greenland: p.56; Celia Chester: pp. 63, 107 (plan); Peter Byatt: p.71 (brochure); Lisa Hall: p.88; Tony Dover for Ibn Battuta: p.95; Rhian Nest James: p.104.

Book design by Peter Ducker MSTD

Solution to exercise 121

9.05   Lucy left the study.
       Trevor phoned Gerald.
9.15   Lucy saw Gerald on the phone.
       Dorothy and Doctor Emerson heard Trevor shouting *at Gerald, on the phone.* When he was checking the accounts he discovered that Gerald had been stealing from the business.
9.25   Doctor Emerson left, banging the front door.
9.30   Gerald entered the house and killed Trevor after a short argument.
9.40   Gerald left the house and met Lucy on her way home.

KEY

1

3 I'm taking
4 I'm staying
5 own
6 I catch
7 I'm making
8 say
9 I understand
10 I help
11 they're harvesting
12 they need
13 I like
14 I'm developing
15 Are you coming
16 I'm spending
17 want
18 It gets
19 you decide
20 you're doing

2

Example answers
4 I am learning to drive
5 My best friend is doing her homework
6 Our next door neighbour is moving house
7 Our teacher is making us work hard
8 Several of my colleagues are taking exams
9 My father is visiting his brother

3

4 is getting
5 have
6 are disappearing
7 are not doing
8 enjoy
9 happens
10 heat
11 melts
12 consist
13 melt
14 believe
15 are already rising
16 includes

4

3 While he was walking in the mountains, Henry saw a bear.
4 The students were playing a game when the professor arrived.
5 Felix phoned the fire brigade when the cooker caught fire.
6 When the starter fired his pistol, the race began.

7 I was walking home when it started to rain.
8 When Margaret opened the door, the phone was ringing.
9 Cora was reading a letter when Jimmy phoned her.
10 Andy came out of the restaurant when he saw Jenny.

5

2 built
3 wasn't selling
4 occupied
5 read
6 was waiting
7 noticed
8 was playing
9 was approaching
10 ran
11 grabbed
12 offered
13 was having
14 had
15 left
16 went

6

3 was having
4 heard
5 contacted
6 invited
7 was organising / organised
8 refused
9 was preparing
10 passed
11 went
12 met
13 was studying
14 had
15 worked
16 were serving
17 announced
18 persuaded
19 was
20 were
21 decided
22 were earning / earned

7

Example answers
2 was working / was eating / was sitting
3 met
4 asked/wanted
5 returned / went back
6 was walking
7 saw/met
8 was visiting
9 met

11 wanted / planned / was planning
12 was looking
13 stole/took
14 was walking / was going
15 began/started
16 decided
17 was getting
18 rang
19 was talking
20 was running
23 decided to go for
24 were looking at
25 dropped a salad / food all over
26 was apologising
27 dropped a pile of pizzas on to
28 didn't have to pay for

8

3 Do you want
4 are getting
5 did you decide
6 were staying
7 we're trying
8 aren't looking
9 don't have
10 We want
11 did
12 lent
13 managed
14 we choose
15 gave
16 was looking

9

2 didn't understand
3 tastes
4 believed
5 doesn't belong
6 are you wearing
7 was jogging
8 contained
9 Do you see
10 prefer
11 were watching

10

4 'm not using
5 're giving
6 'm not going
7 'm trying
8 have
9 see
10 went
11 was shaking

11

Example answers
3 hurts/aches
4 walk/go
5 visited/saw
6 are spending
7 walked/got
8 was coming / was walking
9 began/started
10 am being
11 managed
12 were looking
13 like/want
14 am feeling / feel
15 get

12

3 ... because the engineer <u>didn't call</u> for help ...
4 *right*
5 <u>Is</u> her health <u>improving</u>?
6 <u>I</u> completely <u>agree</u> with you.
7 What did you <u>do</u> after you left school?
8 *right*
9 ... why you <u>believed</u> ...
10 Martin <u>was looking</u> forward to ...
11 *right*
12 Where <u>do you keep</u> ...

13

2 've been coming / 've come
3 've been driving
4 've never had
5 've always been
6 've managed
7 've done / 've been doing
8 've been doing
9 've looked / 've been looking
10 haven't found

14

Example answers
3 've had my hair done. / 've been to the hairdresser.
4 've been chopping onions.
5 've sold my car.
6 've cut my finger!
7 've been going to dancing school. / 've been having lessons.
8 've eaten it all. / 've finished it.

15

2 I've forgotten
3 Have you had
4 he's gone ... He's been having
5 Have you been playing about
6 Have you been studying
7 Have you had
8 he's failed ... He hasn't been working
9 The children have been cooking

10 has Wendy been
11 It's been sitting
12 I've been doing
13 Haven't you bought
14 She's been working
15 I've lost
16 Have you ever played
17 You've been grumbling
18 Your tennis has really improved! ... Have you been practising

16

2 haven't really enjoyed myself since your birthday party.
3 hasn't seen his brother for nearly twenty years.
4 been in Scotland since last Friday. / gone to Scotland.
5 since you rode a bike?
6 been swimming since we were in Spain.
7 weeks since you tidied this room. / been weeks since you tidied this room.

17

2 suits ... have (you) been making
3 don't want ... 've had
4 Have (you) seen
5 has been suffering ... 's been
6 don't know ... hasn't spoken
7 are (you) staring ... haven't seen

18

Example answers
2 'm saving ... go
3 haven't seen ... has he been doing
4 'm staying ... haven't been ... has lived / has been living
5 Have you been waiting
6 don't you rest ... haven't had / haven't taken
7 've been watching
8 's never been ... 's been studying / 's been learning
9 has ... 's having

19

Example answers
2 've been
3 want / 're planning / plan / 've decided
4 're enjoying / 've been enjoying
5 've visited
6 've been wandering / 've been walking
7 haven't spent
8 've taken / 've been taking / 've been getting / 've been doing
9 've had
10 has been
11 say

12 rains
13 've been / 've come
14 guess/suppose

20

Example answers
3 've been
4 do/prepare
5 've seen / 've visited
6 're doing / have
7 are (always) changing
8 makes
9 's gone
10 's been watching
11 looks
12 's (only) come
13 's coming
14 are spending
15 Are you enjoying
16 own/run

21 A

... which I <u>have seen / saw</u> advertised in the local paper.
... when I was twelve and I <u>have lived / have been living</u> here ever since.
I <u>left school three years ago</u> and since then <u>I have had</u> several jobs ...
For the past six months I <u>have been working</u> in Halls ... the manager <u>has said</u> that ...
... I <u>have been learning</u> German ...

21 B

Example answer
Dear Ms Sparks,
    I would like to apply for the job in your shop which I've seen advertised in the paper.
    I am seventeen years old. My first language is Italian, but I also speak quite good German and English. I have not yet left school, but I have some experience in working in a shop, as I sometimes help my uncle who runs a small supermarket.
    My class teacher, Mr Pallini, has said that he is willing to give me a reference.
    I hope you will consider my application.
    Yours sincerely,

22

2 d 3 f 4 a 5 c 6 g 7 e

23

2 did you study ... you qualified
3 did you first meet
4 you've cooked
5 wanted ... weren't

6 has happened ... we've been
  waiting ... hasn't phoned
7 posted ... haven't received

24

3 did you do / was the
4 did you need
5 did you want
6 have you been to / have you
  visited
7 did you do
8 Have you brought / Do you
  have / Did you bring / Have
  you got
9 did you do
10 didn't you do
11 Have you got / Do you have
12 did you become

25

Example answers
3 In the past six months, I've
  done the washing up every
  day.
4 I haven't been windsurfing yet,
  but I hope to one day.
5 Since my last birthday, I've
  been roller-skating every
  Saturday.
6 I haven't eaten a burger
  recently.
7 Last year I broke my leg.
8 Six months ago I passed an
  important exam.
9 I've never ridden a bicycle in
  my life.
10 I sucked my thumb when I was
  a child.
11 I got married yesterday
  evening.
12 This week I've been skiing
  every day.

26

Example answers
3 has been
4 opened
5 has (Neil) had / has (Neil) been
  doing
6 Has (Tina) seen
7 have (you) put
8 spoke
9 has forgotten
10 earned

27

Example answers
4 have been
5 had / have had
6 got/had
7 arrived
8 did (you) have
9 helped
10 didn't

11 liked
12 came/started
13 took
14 've moved / moved
15 hasn't made
16 've made

28

3 took
4 spent
5 have replaced / has replaced
6 have become
7 were
8 has enabled
9 has really improved
10 disappeared
11 took
12 have become
13 have not done
14 has brought
15 has solved

29

3 arrived
4 discovered
5 had reserved
6 did not have
7 had given
8 had also misunderstood
9 required
10 suspected
11 had lost

30

3 *right*
4 ... the play had ended ...
5 ... they hadn't brought ...
6 .... nobody had bought ...
7 ... I found ...
8 ... they had mixed up ...
9 ... I hadn't seen ...
10 ... we decided ...

31

4 I was
5 I'd been waiting / I waited
6 Didn't you get
7 I left
8 I went / I was going
9 I noticed
10 they had changed
11 I put
12 I didn't find
13 it slipped
14 I was waiting
15 what had happened
16 I saw
17 You were laughing
18 I realised
19 you had been sitting
20 I just lost

32

3 had come
4 had cooked
5 had given ... had been working /
  had worked
6 had been worrying
7 had cut
8 had been looking
9 had made

33

2 was (just) leaving / was (just)
  going
3 did
4 didn't
5 said
6 typed / was typing
7 'd (nearly) finished
8 made
9 hadn't given
10 'd been addressing / 'd been
  doing / 'd addressed / 'd done
11 refused

34

1 was working
2 didn't use to be
3 had
4 used to provide
5 was studying
6 rode ... fell

35

3 My aunt used to have a
  dog ...
4 *no change*
5 ... there used to be a football
  pitch ...
6 ... bread didn't use to taste
  like ...
7 ... which used to follow the
  ship ...
8 *no change*
9 The punishments at our school
  used to be very harsh ...
10 ... we used to spend a lot of
  time ... but we didn't use to
  help in the garden.
11 *no change*

36

1 used to enjoy
2 found
3 used to wear
4 Did people really use to think
5 admitted
6 often used to fall
7 were
8 was planning
9 was wearing

37

2   I didn't use to like classical music.
3   I used to be interested in my work.
4   My sister used to borrow my jeans. / My sister used to be thinner.
5   I didn't use to enjoy air travel. / I didn't use to like air travel. / I used to dislike air travel.
6   My brother used to have long hair.
7   I used to smoke.
8   My parents used to live in the USA.
9   My uncle used to be a national swimming champion.
10 We used to live in the town. / We didn't use to be happy.

38

Example answers
3   I used to go to the cinema every Saturday morning when I was small.
4   I didn't use to do my homework until I failed my exams.
5   I used to be very shy, but now I have lots of friends.
6   I used to watch a lot of rubbish on television when I was a kid.
7   I didn't use to wear lipstick when I was a student.
8   I used to work on my grandparents' farm in my school holidays.

39

2   had been hoping
3   had
4   did you live
5   were
6   Do you know
7   used to pass
8   was living
9   Have you written
10 haven't finished
11 I've been trying
12 has been expecting
13 has invited
14 Are you going
15 work
16 did you hear
17 phoned
18 was checking
19 rang
20 told
21 Had you been expecting

40

3   did you visit ... were
4   haven't paid ... do I owe
5   discovered ... had left

6   happened / has happened ... was / used to be ... has lost
7   had ... had been going / was going ... have been sorting
8   spent ... missed / had missed ... were ... had never learnt
9   have always wanted ... have ... have decided

41

1   I'm revising
2   that only lasts
3   I'll get
4   does your evening class finish
5   Shall I come
6   I'm meeting
7   will you talk
8   he won't let
9   I'm playing
10 I'll try
11 he'll agree
12 will you be
13 it stops raining
14 it will go
15 I'll tidy
16 we're waiting

42

2   I'll collect you
3   I'll have to
4   there will probably be
5   the Managing Director is coming
6   We'll be
7   The conference doesn't open
8   I'll make sure
9   I'll read

43

Example answers
3   I'm visiting my cousins in Sardinia. / I'm going to visit ...
4   I'll be happy.
5   I'll eat out with my friends.
6   I'll probably speak quite good English.
7   begins at six o'clock.
8   we're having a class party.
9   finishes on 30th May.

44

2   (I promise) I won't be late.
3   We'll deliver them on Friday.
4   Shall we go to the swimming club?
5   Will you stop fighting!
6   It won't open.
7   Shall I phone for an ambulance? / I'll phone for an ambulance.
8   I won't pay until I've checked them. / I'm not paying ...

45

1   I'm going to be
2   he won't mind
3   I'm going to go
4   Will you hold
5   they're going to raise
6   My car won't start
7   I'm going to start
8   I'll cook

46

4   I'm going to get / I'm getting
5   I'll send
6   I'm going to visit / I'm visiting
7   I'll give
8   Will you
9   I'll go
10 I'm going to see / I'm seeing
11 Will you wash
12 I won't

47

3   people will come
4   I'll phone
5   Shall I phone
6   I'm going to see / I'm seeing
7   Will he give
8   We're going to advertise
9   The bank will lend
10 We'll do
11 he'll help

48

Example answers
2   I'm going to play / I'm playing tennis after work.
3   I'm not going to go / I'm not going abroad this year.
4   (I promise) I'll pay you back at the weekend.
5   Where are you going to go / are you going / are you planning to go / do you plan to go for your honeymoon?
6   Why won't you tell me?
7   I'll have lunch with you but I won't come to see the film because I've already seen it.
8   I'm not going to fail again.
9   Will you turn the volume down please?
10 I'm going to be a film star. / I'm going to appear in a film. / I'm going to be in a film!

49

3   I'm meeting
4   I'll make
5   finishes
6   Shall I bring
7   I'm going to try
8   Will you remember
9   you get
10 I probably won't have

11 my course starts
12 I arrive
13 I'm spending
14 you'll be doing
15 I'll be getting
16 I'll phone
17 I'll be waiting
18 I won't have
19 What are you doing
20 my father is arriving
21 we're having / we're going to have
22 Won't he be
23 he'll be suffering
24 all the family is coming / all the family is going to come
25 I'll be preparing
26 I'm seeing
27 I won't get
28 they close
29 everything goes
30 it'll be / it's going to be
31 the sun shines

50

1 could have phoned
2 could
3 was able
4 haven't been able to find
5 could
6 could
7 couldn't
8 could have been
9 were able to

51

4 He couldn't play tennis. / He wasn't able to play tennis.
5 He couldn't dance. / He wasn't able to dance.
6 He was able to go to the concert.
7 He could listen to music. / He was able to listen to music.
8 He couldn't enter the table tennis competition. / He wasn't able to enter the table tennis competition.

52

(note: may and might are equally acceptable for these sentences)
3 He may/might have slept badly last night.
4 She may/might have dropped something.
5 It may/might be under the bed.
6 They may/might be planning a surprise.
7 He may/might have had some bad news.
8 She may/might be working at home.
9 She may/might have felt tired. /

She may/might have been feeling tired.

53

Example answers
(note: may and might are equally acceptable for these sentences)
3 you may/might get lost.
4 you may/might miss the train.
5 you may/might get fat.
6 she may/might be offended.
7 it may/might break down.
8 you may/might fail it.
9 your boss may/might get angry.
10 you may/might get spots.

54

1 must be
2 must have been
3 can't be
4 can't be
5 may be having
6 can't have enjoyed
7 may be delivering
8 can't have been concentrating
9 must be

55

3 have met
4 know
5 be
6 have sold
7 be
8 have lent

56

(note: may and might are equally acceptable for 4, 6 and 8)
3 can't be hers.
4 may/might be in the car/office.
5 must/might have been a present.
6 may/might not have seen you. / can't have seen you.
7 can't have done.
8 may/might have been his brother/father/cousin ... can't have been Peter.

57

1 d   2 c   3 f   4 e   5 a   6 b

58

Example answers
3 Kay must have changed her mind about marrying him.
4 A pickpocket may/might have stolen it.
5 She must/may/might be renting it from him.
6 It must be a bomb!
7 It may/might have been sent by my brother.

8 She must have been held up (in the traffic).

59

1 Must we do
2 should have posted
3 should be
4 must have missed
5 needn't have bothered
6 ought to
7 don't have to
8 should arrive
9 must have got lost

60

1 must
2 needn't
3 Shouldn't
4 shouldn't
5 needn't
6 mustn't
7 should
8 needn't
9 should

61

1 c   2 e   3 a   4 d   5 f   6 g
7 b

62

2 should get the contract.
3 needn't / don't need to / don't have to spend a long time at the museum if it's not interesting.
4 shouldn't have spoken to my mother like that.
5 should have phoned me
6 needn't have made / didn't need to make
7 mustn't find out what I've done.
8 should move house now.
9 didn't have to / didn't need to call a taxi.
10 should check the timetable before we leave.

63

3 *no change*
4 ... you'd better ask permission.
5 *no change*
6 ... I'd better explain ...
7 They'd better not go ...
8 *no change*

64

2 'd better / should
3 have to
4 should
5 have to
6 'd better / should
7 should
8 should

9 have to
10 'd better / should
11 have to
12 should
13 'd better / should

65

2 should check all the windows are shut whenever you go out.
3 shouldn't borrow money from people you hardly know.
4 had better / should keep the door shut in case someone sees us.
5 have to train regularly if you want to succeed in athletics.
6 had better not / shouldn't wear that bracelet to school.
7 don't have to pay extra for delivery.
8 had better / should pick those tomatoes before they get too ripe.

66

3 ought to have visited me.
4 ought not to have used it. / ought to have asked his permission.
5 ought to pick it.
6 ought not to be playing with matches.
7 ought to be an instruction leaflet.
8 ought to have phoned her.

67

Example answers
2 should resign. / resign. / resigned.
3 should take more exercise. / take more exercise. / took more exercise.
4 should have a new car. / has a new car.
5 should./does.
6 should work harder. / work harder.

68

1 he sees / he should see / he see
2 I shouldn't bother / I wouldn't bother
3 I check / I should check
4 should Gareth call / if Gareth calls / if Gareth should call
5 should I do / shall I do
6 they should disappear
7 I search / I should search
8 we should wait / we wait
9 we should rent / we rent
10 they should be / they are

69

1 We were very surprised that Tom should behave / behaved in such a rude manner.
2 I asked a shop assistant for directions and he recommended trying the tourist information office. *or* he recommended (that) I should try... *or* he recommended (that) I try ...
3 *right*
4 If I can't leave my bags here, what do you suggest I should do with them *or* what do you suggest I do with them?
5 *right* (*wouldn't* would also be acceptable)
6 *not a question so no question mark needed.*

70

1 I miss
2 doesn't arrive
3 won't refund
4 you reach
5 will you cut
6 Would you work
7 didn't complain
8 I've checked
9 Wouldn't my friends be

71

2 he didn't like
3 You'll find
4 Wouldn't your parents be proud
5 I don't revise
6 would you look for
7 you weren't
8 would you feel
9 you could

72

Example answers
2 (How) much would you earn (if) you got it?
3 Would it help (if) I lent you some?
4 (What) colour would you paint it (if) you re-decorated?
5 (What) will happen (if) you fail / ... (if) you don't pass?

73

2 If you found a job abroad/ if you could find a job abroad, would you take it?
3 If it were/was somewhere I want/wanted to go, I'd certainly consider it carefully.
4 I'd only consider that if I were/was sure about the family.
5 If they didn't treat me well, I'd be very miserable.

6 You'd have to be sure to use a reputable agency. / You have to be sure ...
7 I will/can/could get you one if you're interested.
8 if I decided to apply, would you give me a reference? / if I decide to apply, will you give me a reference?

74

Example answers
2 What would you do if you won a lottery prize?
3 What would you do if you saw someone being mugged?
4 What would you do if your house was on fire?
5 What would you do if you were having a problem with grammar?
6 How would your father react if you left school?
7 What would happen if your teacher stepped on a banana skin?
8 What would happen if you overslept?
9 What would you and your friends do if you didn't have to earn money?
10 What would happen to car manufacturers if we all rode bicycles?
11 What would happen if all the politicians retired?

75

Your answers should have the same structures as those in 74.

76

1 e 2 f 3 a 4 b 5 g 6 c 7 d

77

Example answers
2 (I) wouldn't work here (if) I were/was
3 (If) I'd realised, I wouldn't have asked her about him.
4 (You) wouldn't have hurt yourself (if) you'd been looking where you were going.
5 (If) you'd known I was coming, would you have brought one for me?
6 (Would) you still love me (if) I was/were poor? ... (if) I wasn't/weren't joking, what would you say? *or* (But if) I had (really) lost all my money what would you say/do?

78

Example answers

2 If they hadn't cancelled so late, the travel company would have given them a refund.
3 If the travel agent hadn't failed his final exam when he was a student, he wouldn't have felt sorry for Cherry.
4 If he hadn't had a cancellation on a tour which started later in the summer, he wouldn't have been able to transfer her booking.
5 If the booking hadn't been transferred, her father's money would have been wasted.
6 If they hadn't had a row, his girlfriend would have been with him.
7 If they hadn't been the only ones travelling alone, they wouldn't have found themselves going round the sights together.
8 If he had read about the places they were visiting, she wouldn't have spent most of her time telling him about them.
9 If she hadn't failed that exam she wouldn't have met her future husband.

79

Example answers

3 I wouldn't be able to play for my friends if I hadn't practised.
4 If I'd come home earlier, I wouldn't be so sleepy.
5 I'd be able to concentrate if I'd had some breakfast.
6 If I'd remembered to book seats last week, we could have gone to the concert. / ... we could go to the concert.
7 I wouldn't have been fired if I hadn't missed the bus.
8 I wouldn't have run out of petrol if I'd stopped to buy some.

80

Example answers

5 hadn't eaten so much.
6 would be more popular.
7 didn't come to your party?
8 pressed this button?
9 wouldn't have got arrested. / wouldn't be in this mess.
10 would you do it?
11 don't give them any. / you mustn't give them any.
12 you had run out of money?
13 will you give him a message?
14 borrowed their bikes.

15 gets some fresh air.
16 what would you have said?
20 If I had more free time, I would take more exercise.
21 If people had realised that smoking was dangerous when they were young they wouldn't be having serious health problems now ...
22 The first motorways might/would never have been built if more people had been concerned about pollution in the 1960s.
23 The seeds wouldn't have died if the schoolchildren had remembered to water them *or* The seeds would have grown if the schoolchildren hadn't forgotten to water them. *or* ... if the schoolchildren had watered them.
24 If we don't protect wildlife now, there will be nothing left for future generations.
25 If people realised how important it is to conserve energy, they might/would do something about it.
26 If poor farmers weren't encouraged to grow crops to sell instead of food, they wouldn't have problems feeding ...

81

3 I wish I had a car.
4 I wish I worked in an office. / I wish I was/were working in an office.
5 I wish I lived with my son. / I wish I was/were living with my son.
6 I wish I could swim.
7 I wish I hadn't listened to the hairdresser.
8 I wish I didn't live in the city.
9 I wish I were/was a helicopter pilot.
10 I wish I'd worked harder.

82

Example answers

MARTIN:
I wish he'd wash his coffee cup.
I wish he wouldn't leave dirty clothes around the room.
I wish he wouldn't come in late.
I wish he wouldn't lie in bed watching television.

BERNIE:
I wish he'd tell me what's wrong.
I wish he wouldn't sulk.

I wish he wouldn't interfere with my possessions.
I wish he wouldn't move my books around.

83

Example answers

2 wish I was/were as rich as James. / wish I was/were rich.
3 wish I'd had dancing lessons / wish I had learned to dance
4 wish I'd known.
5 wishes they hadn't moved. / wishes they could move back again.
6 they wish they'd never started.

84

2 was written by George Orwell.
3 were built by the Ancient Egyptians.
4 was invented by Guglielmo Marconi.
5 was painted by Picasso.
6 was designed by Gustave Eiffel.
7 was discovered by Crick and Watson.

85

3 The businessman has been robbed.
4 She's been asked out. / She has been asked out.
5 The dishes have been washed.
6 The puncture has been mended.
7 He's retired. / He has retired.
8 Jane Jones has been elected.
9 He's been stung. / He has been stung.
10 The rabbit has disappeared.
11 He's been arrested. / He has been arrested.
12 They've passed.

86

2 Nearly £50,000 was taken from the hotel safe.
3 Several of the bedrooms were also broken into.
4 Articles of value were removed.
5 Several pieces of equipment were damaged.
6 and 7 The chef was injured and was left lying unconscious on the floor.
8 The thieves were arrested early this morning.

87

1 are/will be needed ... be signed?
2 can't/won't be overheard.
3 wouldn't have been sacked.
4 is never answered ... are kept ... have been written

5 had been watered ... had been cut
6 ... is suspected ... has been arrested ... is being questioned ... can/will be identified
7 was being re-organised ... had been moved

88

1 ... her new grandson who <u>was born</u> last week.
2 ... because <u>it belonged</u> to my grandmother.
3 *right*
4 ... my camera. <u>It's being repaired</u> this week.
5 The bridge <u>collapsed</u> during the floods ...
6 ... someone <u>will get hurt</u> in a minute. *or* ... <u>will be hurt</u> ...
7 ... but it <u>didn't refer</u> to you.
8 *right*
9 ... the money <u>had disappeared</u>?
10 Children under the age of seven <u>are not allowed</u> in this pool.

89

1 got
2 will get
3 is
4 got
5 got
6 were/are
7 gets
8 got
9 are
10 got

90

2 was kept waiting for half an hour by the bank manager.
3 must be paid by employers.
4 could have been written by your brother?
5 is used to do that job nowadays.
6 were being made redundant by the firm almost every week.
7 were not informed that there had been a mistake.
8 be sent by your company next year?
9 was distressed by the news about the famine.
10 hasn't been claimed.
11 ever been asked for your opinion?
12 shouldn't have been opened by the children.
13 must be worn by all visitors.

91

1 got stuck / was stuck
2 is closed / has been closed
3 is completed / has been completed
4 be finished
5 will be opened / is going to be opened / is being opened
6 has been invited
7 will have been wasted / is going to be wasted / will be wasted
8 have been planted / were planted
9 were ignored
10 should have been spent
11 were elected
12 will be thrown

92

1 have been taken / were taken
2 were introduced / have been introduced
3 made / have made
4 were shown
5 has belonged
6 was given
7 was killed
8 suffered / had suffered
9 was restored
10 added
11 doesn't feel
12 happened / had happened
13 was sent / had been sent
14 behaved / had behaved
15 be sacked / get sacked
16 is invited / will be invited

93

2 was seen
3 was going
4 saw
5 had been told / had been asked
6 was asked
7 didn't know
8 was told
9 won't do
10 will do
11 has had / has been asked
12 be done

94

3 has been closed.
4 was being used
5 has been built
6 were playing
7 was building
8 is being built
9 was polluted
10 have been caught

95

2 ... I'm going to have my number changed.

3 ... she should be having the plaster taken off ...
4 ... he's had a fine new house designed.
5 ... I'm having blinds fitted on the windows.
6 ... she had him followed.
7 ... he'd had his portrait painted ...
8 ... to have it straightened.

96

2 Do you live locally?
3 What is your address? / Where do you live?
4 When did you leave school?
5 Which school did you go to?
6 Are you working now?
7 Who do you work for?
8 How long have you been working there / for them? *or* How long have you worked there / for them?
9 Do you enjoy your present job?
10 Why do you want to leave?

97

2 Is one with a sea view available?
3 have you heard about the special offer we are running at the moment?
4 Why don't you take advantage of it?
5 What do I have to do to qualify for it?
6 How much would that be?
7 Who should I make the cheque payable to?

98

2 how much do you weigh? / what do you weigh?
3 how tall are you?
4 What do you do (for a living) / What's your job/occupation?
5 do you take regular exercise?
6 Do you do any sport? / Do you take part in any sport?
7 Do you smoke?
8 Have you (ever) tried to give (it) up?

99

Example answers
2 how much this jacket costs? / how much this jacket is?
3 where the books about Russia are.
4 what time the last bus leaves? / when the last bus leaves?
5 how to use this coffee machine? / how this coffee machine works?

6 why the car has stopped. / why the car won't go.

7 where the manager's office is?

8 when the first Olympic Games took place?

9 how old your sister is.

100

1 Have <u>you ever</u> been to Thailand?

2 What <u>does</u> this word <u>mean</u>?

3 How much <u>does it cost</u> to fly to Australia from here?

4 We can't remember where <u>we put</u> our passports.

5 *right*

6 Would you like to explain what <u>the problem is</u>?

7 How long did it <u>take you</u> to get here?

8 Now I understand why <u>you didn't</u> tell me about your job!

9 *right*

10 Why <u>don't people in your country</u> show more respect to the elderly?

101

Rachel said

2 she worked for a small publishing company.

3 she was their marketing manager.

4 the company had opened an office in Barcelona.

5 it had been very successful.

6 she had been chosen to run a new office in Madrid.

7 she was studying Spanish in the evenings.

8 she didn't have much time to enjoy herself.

9 she hadn't had lunch with a friend for ages.

10 she hoped all her friends would come and visit her in Madrid.

11 she had been there the week before with her secretary.

12 they hadn't had much time for sightseeing.

13 she had to get back to work.

102

She said

3 I'd obviously been ill for days.

4 I couldn't go to work.

5 I'm much too thin.

6 I don't/didn't eat sensibly.

7 I needed to stay in bed.

8 I don't keep my flat warm enough.

9 I'd got a nasty cough.

10 I could phone her if I felt worse.

11 I'd feel better in a few days.

12 I need a good holiday.

103

2 was upset

3 wasn't interested

4 had promised to meet her / promised to meet her

5 hadn't turned up / didn't turn up

6 didn't want to see you

7 was a telephone

8 didn't believe you had tried. / didn't believe you tried.

9 she would talk to you.

10 was going to be late for work

104

2 ... a disco was held every night.

3 ... said you could go horse-riding.

4 He said room service was available.

5 He said they served an international menu in the dining-room.

6 He said a fitness centre had been added to the hotel's facilities.

7 He said the tennis courts could be booked free of charge.

8 He said the gardens had a wonderful variety of flowers.

9 He said I'd love the private beach.

10 He said guests could use the nearby golf course free of charge.

105

2 if/whether I lived locally.

3 my address. / what my address was. / where I lived.

4 when I left school. / when I had left school.

5 which school I'd gone/been to. / which school I went to.

6 if/whether I was working now.

7 who I worked for.

8 how long I'd been working there. / how long I'd been working for them. / how long I worked ...

9 if/whether I enjoyed my present job.

10 why I wanted to leave.

106

2 (me) where I was going to spend the holiday.

3 (me) what I would do when I left school.

4 how the doctor knew her name.

5 (me) whether/if I had an appointment.

6 whether/if his wife had seen his car keys.

7 why she hadn't phoned him.

8 James to carry his briefcase.

9 the receptionist when he could see the doctor.

107

2 'Where do you come from?'

3 'I come from Dublin.'

4 'That's where I was born too.'

5 'I've been a fan of yours for ages.'

6 'I'm very flattered.'

7 'Are you going to the concert tonight?'

8 'We want to, but we haven't been able to get tickets, because they've sold all but the most expensive ones and we can't afford those.'

9 'Can they have some at the cheaper price?'

108

2 did you say

3 tell

4 to tell

5 would you say

6 to say

7 told us / said

8 told

9 wouldn't say

10 won't say

11 've already told

12 tell me / say

13 tell

109

2 told

3 said

4 told

5 had said

6 to tell

7 said

8 Tell

9 was saying

110

1 ... she had lost her job and <u>was</u> short of money. / she <u>has lost</u> her job and <u>is</u> ...

2 *right*

3 She <u>was telling us</u> about her fascinating trip ... / ... was <u>talking</u> about ...

4 *right*

5 ... the receptionist <u>told us that</u> the hotel ... / ... <u>said that</u> the hotel ...

6 ... visitors <u>not to touch</u> the exhibits.
7 *right (if it is still true) or* ... the castle <u>was</u> only open ... *(whether it's still true or not)*

111

3 interrupting
4 to meet
5 spending
6 entering
7 to speak
8 living
9 lifting
10 to bring
11 to be living
12 working
13 to support
14 being delayed
15 explaining

112

2 to see / to visit
3 postponing / putting off
4 painting/decorating
5 going/changing
6 to deliver
7 to send / to post
8 to do / to post
9 losing/offending
10 writing
11 to help
12 to join
13 going
14 speaking/replying/talking

113

2 to ride
3 to give
4 setting
5 to lose
6 hitting
7 crashing
8 to try
9 losing / having lost
10 to raise
11 to be helped
12 to find

114

2 Jason to sit.
3 Roger Hopkins to hand over the money.
4 buying Della the drums. / buying them (for her).
5 Charlie finish his homework / Charlie finish it.
6 to reach the shampoo.
7 washing. / to be washed.
8 Sandra (to) lay the table.
9 making the mess. / having made the mess.
10 cleaning windows.
11 Betty to join them.

115

2 to speak
3 being shouted
4 to sack
5 to have worked
6 changing
7 whether to say
8 being
9 to get
10 to pass
11 anybody/anyone help
12 to discuss
13 asking
14 to have known

116

Example answers
2 I learnt <u>to swim</u> at the age of <u>six.</u>
3 I can't help <u>crying</u> when ...
4 I don't practise <u>speaking English</u> as ...
5 I sometimes pretend <u>to be listening</u> when ...
6 I always encourage <u>people to read books</u> which ...
7 I remember <u>going to the circus</u> ..., but I don't remember <u>enjoying it</u>, although ...
8 I enjoy <u>swimming</u> even though I'm not ...
9 I expect <u>to have left school</u> by the end ...
10 I've given up <u>going to discos,</u> because they're too noisy.
11 I often help <u>to prepare lunch at weekends.</u>

117 A

2 a 3 f 4 c 5 g 6 e 7 d

117 B

2 by checking the instructions.
3 spending too long on one question.
4 time trying to see how your friends are getting on.
5 by allowing time to check all your answers.
6 cheating, in the long run.

118

Example answers
2 sitting at home.
3 asking their permission.
4 offering to help you.
5 helping people who don't want it.
6 having any proof.
7 being late.
8 starting a long journey.

119

3 go
4 waking
5 arrive
6 finding
7 spending
8 say
9 being

120

3 of looking
4 to risk
5 in persuading
6 to hearing
7 to have
8 to achieve
9 for letting / to have let
10 of sending
11 in going

121

4 had been murdered
5 didn't love
6 didn't murder
7 wanted
8 had / was having
9 asked
10 was watching
11 told
12 called
13 noticed
14 had expected / had been expecting
15 answered
16 was still shouting
17 were obviously having
18 took
19 shouting
20 had gone
21 to go
22 didn't want
23 heard
24 came
25 was still talking
26 heard
27 wasn't shouting
28 phoned
29 talked
30 told
31 had decided

32 was watching
33 take
34 spilt
35 was pouring
36 didn't want
37 crept
38 decided
39 never like
40 talk / am talking
41 had had
42 normally takes
43 took
44 went

45 saw
46 was walking
47 saw
48 was standing
49 didn't see / couldn't see
50 was talking
51 didn't answer
52 remembered
53 had told / told
54 was playing / was going to play
55 walked
56 met
57 reached
58 was looking

59 called
60 was
61 had planned
62 had been visiting
63 let
64 seemed
65 showed
66 shouting
67 were having / had been having
68 stopped
69 went
70 had already left
71 got
72 to explain
73 to have
74 didn't let / wouldn't let
75 was
76 didn't know
77 was talking
78 realised
79 arguing
80 left
81 seeing

82 weren't
83 is
84 've lived / 've been living
85 used to have / had
86 bought
87 earning / to earn
88 went
89 went
90 lost
91 was looking
92 met
93 was walking
94 seemed
95 had seen
96 hadn't
97 went
98 found

99 can't have been / wasn't
100 didn't even go
101 had found out
102 means
103 left / must have left

104 was going to leave / was leaving
105 to murder
106 didn't walk / can't have walked / couldn't have walked
107 met
108 was still being shouted at
109 has been telling / is telling
110 made

122

3 <u>a</u> biscuit
4 *no change*
5 <u>an</u> omelette
6 *no change*
7 *no change*
9 a burger
10 a bowl of soup / soup
11 cheese
12 a banana
13 a coffee / coffee
14 cream

123

3 ... the <u>traffic is</u> terrible.
4 ... because <u>of bad behaviour</u> ...
5 *right*
6 ... Rebecca had her <u>hair</u> cut short ...
7 ... the <u>furniture takes</u> up too much space.
8 ... I give you <u>some advice?</u> / ... <u>a piece of advice</u>?
9 *right*
10 ... was <u>a less unpleasant experience</u> than I had expected.

124

3 room
4 experience
5 scenery
6 weather
7 day
8 rooms
9 paper
10 experiences
11 views
12 papers

125

3	a	11	a
4	some	12	a
5	the	13	a
6	a	14	some
7	a	15	the
8	the	16	the
9	The	17	an
10	the		

Example answers
18 In the kitchen there is a stove with a frying-pan on it.
19 There's an egg in the frying-pan.

126

2	the	8	The
3	the	9	the
4	a	10	a
5	a	11	a
6	the	12	the
7	a		

127

4	The	12	–
5	the	13	the
6	–	14	–
7	–	15	the
8	the	16	–
9	the	17	the
10	the	18	–
11	–	19	the

128

... and ~~the~~ Malaysia and then go on to the Philippines, where he will make a speech about the environment.

~~The~~ King Juan Carlos of ~~the~~ Spain arrived in London today for a three day visit to the United Kingdom. He was met by the Queen and drove with her to ~~the~~ Buckingham Palace. Tomorrow he will have ~~the~~ lunch with the Governor of the Bank of England and in the evening he will have talks with ~~the~~ businessmen.

A conference is taking place in ~~the~~ Mexico City on ways of helping the unemployed in the developing world. A report will be sent to the United Nations, but it is feared that ~~the~~ unemployment will remain a problem in ~~the~~ most countries for many years to come.

129

Example answers
5 of them were wearing shorts.
6 of them had socks.
7 (of) the men have/had beards.
8 (of) the men have/had short hair.
9 (of) the men were wearing belts.
10 of the men was wearing sunglasses.
11 of the men had a jacket. / of the men was wearing a jacket.
12 of the men was carrying a newspaper.

130

Example answers
5 All of my friends live in the city.

6 Lots of our neighbours have pets.
7 All politicians are ambitious.
8 Some of my cousins are very poor.
9 Neither of my parents enjoys/enjoy noisy parties.

131
2 none of
3 Few/Most (!)
4 half (of) ... all of ... any of ...
5 most ... a few
6 much
7 each

132
2 anything
3 All
4 both
5 none of the
6 them
7 every morning
8 Neither of
9 somebody
10 somewhere
11 little
12 a few
13 no
14 anywhere
15 The whole
16 nothing

133
3 ... if anybody gets left ...
4 There are no good restaurants, nothing!
5 ... he had few friends ...
6 right
7 ... because all the information
8 ... I could have any seat ...
9 ... because I have none. / ... I haven't any. /... I haven't got any.
10 ... I have a lot of homework ... / ... I have got a lot of homework ...
11 right
12 ... embarrassed that everyone knows my problem. / ... that everybody knows my problem.

134
2 Antonio Stradivari was an Italian who made wonderful violins.
3 Ibn Battuta was a Moroccan who travelled through Africa and Asia.
4 Johann Gutenberg was a German who constructed the first mechanical printing press.
5 Joseph Lister was an Englishman who began the use

of antiseptics in operating theatres.
6 Orville Wright was an American who flew the first real aeroplane.
7 Joseph Niepce was a Frenchman who produced the first permanent photograph.

135
3	whose	8	–
4	who/that	9	–
5	–	10	that
6	–	11	–
7	where	12	where

136 A
3 a 4 a 5 b 6 a 7 b
8 a 9 b 10 a

136 B
Example answers
3 b I have one aunt. She lives in New York. She is getting married.
4 b Peter made the sandwiches. There is some cake too. The sandwiches have been eaten, but there is some cake left.
5 a There are several parks. We used to play in one. It's been built over, but the others are still there.
6 b Our school has one French teacher. He lives near my house. He helps me with my homework.

137
Example answers
3 where you have to wear a tie.
4 who enjoy rock music.
5 which aren't in fashion.
6 which have plenty of action.
7 whose parents argue.
8 to whom I can say anything.

138
2 really good cook.
3 extremely foolishly.
4 very friendly to(wards) us.
5 practical (to me).
6 hard.
7 well today?
8 a fast swimmer.

139
2 good
3 efficiently
4 hard
5 surprisingly
6 quickly
7 lately
8 fluent

9 near
10 pleasant
11 busy
12 easily
13 different
14 absolutely
15 good
16 accurate

140
3 seemed unnecessarily complicated ...
4 if you tried hard.
5 *right*
6 she speaks perfect French.
7 an exceptionally demanding job.
8 she's well enough ...
9 *right*
10 a very well-paid job.

141
2 the lowest
3 better than
4 worse than / not as well as / not so well as
5 higher ... than
6 less
7 the same ... as
8 more than
9 less than

Example answers
13 Jill collected more than Alex or Wayne.
14 Bronwen collected the same amount as Jill.
15 Wayne collected the least paper.
16 Alex didn't collect as much as Bronwen, but he collected more than Wayne.
17 Jill collected twenty kilos less than Flora, but five kilos more than Alex.

142
5 much easier than
6 the best
7 the highest mountain
8 farther/further north than
9 not as warm as / not so warm as
10 later
11 earlier here than
12 any faster
13 as fast as
14 shorter than I am
15 (any) better
16 worse
17 as much money as / so much money as

143

3 Craig has occasionally offered to work through lunch.
4 Angela isn't usually in the office at lunch-time.
5 John won't usually do overtime.
6 Craig usually leaves later than everyone else.
7 Angela has hardly ever taken a day off.
8 John hardly ever has sandwiches for lunch.
9 Craig is hardly ever ill.

144

3 Well, the downstairs ones are always locked.
4 We even have a lock on the little one in the hall.
5 Well, I think most of the windows were probably locked.
6 They were all locked on Friday.
7 I knew we would both be out all day.
8 I definitely didn't.

145

3 was probably bored.
4 has never been there.
5 often has a rest about this time.
6 has almost finished it.
7 hasn't even been invited.
8 both want to marry Alice.

146

2 By
3 during
4 until
5 at … in
6 –
7 in
8 until
9 on
10 in
11 by
12 in
13 at
14 on

147

3 For
4 until
5 By/At
6 During/In
7 by
8 in
9 for/–
10 at
11 during

148

3 At
4 until
5 in
6 at/by
7 at
8 for
9 during
10 on
11 until
12 by
13 at
14 at
15 by

149

2 at
3 in
4 in
5 on
6 at
7 In
8 at
9 in
10 at
11 to
12 on
13 at

150

2 on
3 in
4 at
5 on
6 at
7 in
8 in
9 on

151

2 of
3 to
4 to
5 for
6 with
7 in
8 for
9 on
10 on
11 as
12 with

152

3 in the shade.
4 on a diet.
5 by credit card.
6 by plane.
7 by little-known Russian artists.
8 at 130 kilometres an hour.
9 in capital letters.
10 on the phone.
11 on the whole.
12 as my best friend.

13 by a wasp.
14 like the last one.
15 by the photocopier.
16 as a motorcycle messenger.
17 in the fog.
18 in love.

153

5 … very proud of her son …
6 … interested in folk music.
7 *right*
8 … threw a bottle at the car …
9 … they'd never heard of such a person.
10 … before he leaves for the office in the morning.
11 *right*
12 … do anything about it.
13 … who believes in saying what he thinks …
14 … searched the car for drugs.
15 … bored with this exercise …
16 *right*
17 … shocked at/by what I said.
18 … he had apologised to me …

154 A

2 f 3 e 4 c 5 d 6 a

154 B

1 b 2 e 3 a 4 f 5 c 6 d

155

2 up (with her).
3 out (of them).
4 it up.
5 on with it.
6 it up
7 us down
8 on with them

156

3 I only went in for it for a joke.
4 Unless you own up we shall all be punished.
5 … please think it over very carefully.
6 We can't carry on if you won't co-operate.
7 … she stood up for it vigorously.
8 … but he turned it down …
9 … because we couldn't put up with the noise …
10 … when his boss found out what he had been doing.

157

1 + s
bricks
plays
moths
ghosts
guys

2 + es
kisses
taxes
buses
brushes
marches

3 ~~y~~ + ies
spies
parties
berries
queries
ponies

158

1 + ing
chattering
failing
worrying
freeing
planting
replying
despairing
staying
widening
considering

2 ~~e~~ + ing
staring
loving
refusing
invading

3 double letter + ing
rebelling
referring
admitting
swimming
rubbing